SWINDON
DECODED

the curious history around us

JOHN CHANDLER

For Roger Trayhurn, in recognition of more than forty years' distinguished service to the people of Swindon and their history

First published in 1992, as *Swindon: history and guide*, by Alan Sutton Publishing. This revised and expanded edition published in the United Kingdom in 2005 by The Hobnob Press, PO Box 1838, East Knoyle, Salisbury SP3 6FA

British Library Cataloguing in Publication Data
A catalogue record for this book is available from the British Library.

ISBN 0-946418-37-3

Typeset in ITC Officina Serif and Futura
Typesetting, photography and origination by John Chandler
Printed in Great Britain by Salisbury Printing Company Ltd, Salisbury

DR JOHN CHANDLER has been involved in the history of Wiltshire since the 1970s, and has written histories of Salisbury, the Vale of Pewsey, Wiltshire churches, and Shaftesbury, among more than twenty books about aspects of local and regional history. He has been general editor of the Wiltshire Record Society and co-editor of the *Wiltshire Archaeological and Natural History Magazine*. He runs Hobnob Press from his home in south Wiltshire, and is working on a history of the whole county, of which two volumes (covering Kennet District) have been published so far. The volume on Swindon and North-Eastern Wiltshire is in preparation.

CONTENTS

INTRODUCTION

DOWN THERE alongside Basingstoke and Bognor, Scunthorpe and Wigan, Swindon is a place to be made fun of – clone town, crap town, handy town whenever a London journalist, short on originality, needs somewhere to be rude about.

But why? Is it the name? Well admittedly Swindon probably does mean 'pig hill'. And yes, viewed from the rest of Wiltshire Swindon does have a kind of alien quality – a form of civilization, but not as others know it.

I first became acquainted with Swindon over three decades ago, when I worked for a year in the central reference library in Regent Circus. I have fondish memories of the place, particularly of the evening shift (we were open until 9 in those days). There were the old men after 'yesterday's Adver" (they weren't allowed to read the current issue, so always had their local news a day late), rock concert rehearsals going on in the room upstairs while we were trying to keep the peace, innocent flirting with the library assistants, and attempting (just as inexpertly, and once with painful consequences) to eject drunks.

And yet that year also nurtured in me an affection and respect for the place, born out of curiosity, I suppose. The civic pride was palpable; there was that no-nonsense dignity of a workaday town that could produce solid, heavy, complicated machines; and there were mysterious new industries arriving – polymers and electronics – bowled along by the recently completed motorway.

But there was also something wrong. I remember strolling out on my first lunch-break and looking for the town centre. There didn't seem to be one. Towns I was used to had a square with a church nearby and busy streets leading in from all directions. Nothing like that here. Of course a few days later I discovered such a place, up on the hill, but it was nowhere near what I perceived to be the centre – decidedly eccentric, in fact.

Perhaps it was that observation that started me on a lifetime's interest in urban topography – the shape, history and growth of towns. How, merely by looking around and some historical detective work, can we make sense of the places where we live? Years later, with several town histories to my name and others in progress, I was approached by a publisher to write a short history of, and guide to, a Wiltshire town. Swindon seemed my obvious choice. It was published in 1992, sold modestly, was well reviewed, languished for a while, and then (not for the first or last time in my career) I ended up buying all the unsold copies for a pittance, and flogging them myself.

A shame, I thought, and as authors always do, I blamed the publisher. Now that I am a publisher myself no-one can stop me trying again. Swindon's history is extraordinary, weird, unique; but it is like a code, needing a key to decipher it. Writing about it made me a Swindon enthusiast. And maybe reading about it will make you one too. Because, after all, like any town Swindon needs people to understand it and become enthusiastic about it. So I have returned to my 1992 book, shaken it up, changed and added and subtracted, brought it up to date, and reassembled it. And here it is.

Well, I LIKE Swindon – and I am not alone. If you don't, maybe you just have not understood why it is the way it is. Read my book and you will find out.

JOHN CHANDLER
November 2005

1 SWINDON LAND- SCAPES

S WINDON is best approached from the south. Driving up from Devizes, after many miles of downland the traveller begins to descend, and a different world is suddenly revealed. Beyond the flat green patchwork of Wroughton's rectangular fields and the incessant motorway there are houses and factories, office blocks and warehouses, a church spire and a hospital. Go up there and sit in that lay-by where the view begins and you can watch Swindon wake up. It is 7 o'clock on a spring morning, and the sun is

dissolving a light lingering mist in preparation for another hot day. With binoculars you can make out the hazy outline of higher ground, the Corallian ridge on which Purton, Blunsdon and Stratton are perched, and you can see that in places the houses extend up to and over this temporary horizon. Later the mist will clear, to reveal Braydon Forest and the Cotswolds beyond. In front of you a broad low hill rises from the valley to mask the longer view; it was this limestone eminence which gave Swindon its name, and it was here that Old Swindon, or High Swindon, was built. To its right you can make out more offices and factories, and you know that behind them is rolled a carpet of houses far further than the eye can see.

A statue of Swindon native, Diana Dors, presides over a disabled car park at the West Swindon neighbourhood centre

Of the many hundreds of buildings discernible through the mist perhaps only a dozen are more than 150 years old, and they are almost all outside Swindon – at Wroughton and Elcombe in the foreground. Away to the left Toothill, Freshbrook and the other West Swindon neighbourhoods have all arrived since I occasionally used to cycle along there to work from Wootton Bassett thirty years ago. Swindon itself had a population below 2,000 until about 1840; now, including Stratton, it has just about reached 200,000, a hundredfold increase. – Remarkable! Perhaps, therefore, this book should begin in 1840.

But that would be quite wrong. The landscape itself, on which modern Swindon so recently sits, has been shaped and modified by men and women since prehistory, and here and there (and more than most people imagine) traces of their handiwork show through. This chapter examines the landscapes of greater Swindon, from their geological origins through centuries of agriculture and rural settlement, up to the point at which they became 'Swindonized'. In chapters two and three we shall look at the successive communities which have lived at the heart of these landscapes, on Swindon Hill itself; and from chapter four onwards we shall enter the world of railways, suburbs and urban life generally, the Swindon which we know today.

Southern England's terrain results from a sequence of rocks formed as sediment on the ocean floor. The chemical composition of each stratum depends on various factors, including the nature of the riverborne material being carried into the ocean at the time, and the organisms which the water could sustain. Geological forces have buckled the strata, and climatic forces have eroded them, so that different rocks break the land surface in different places, and have succumbed in various ways to the effects of water, frost and vegetation. A line drawn on a map across the Swindon area, from Chiseldon in the south-east to Cricklade in the north-west, represents a journey back through geological time, as different rocks are encountered, each older than the one before. The downland above Chiseldon and Wroughton, around the lay-by where I have absent-mindedly left you sitting, is made of Chalk, the youngest rock in the sequence. Below this Chalk the line traverses Greensands and Clays, then the Corallian Limestone, then older Clays beyond. Because of their different properties the rocks manifest themselves in different ways – the Chalk as well-drained rounded hills, the heavy Clays as flat valleys,

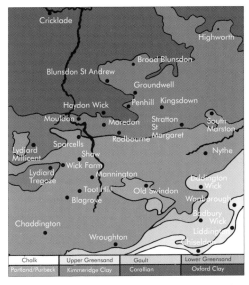

The simplified geology of the Swindon area

often waterlogged, the Limestone as an irregular ridge, and so on.

This over-simplification explains much of the landscape structure seen from the lay-by above Wroughton. But it does not account for Swindon Hill, which at its western limit (near the site of the former Princess Margaret Hospital) stands up proud from the clay, and which extends eastwards almost to the chalk beyond Broome. This hill is largely composed of Portland and Purbeck Beds, fine building Limestones which occur also in south Wiltshire and Dorset. Their presence here is explained by a syncline, or concave fold, in the Clay at this point, which beneath the ocean filled up with deep deposits of shelly sediment. The deposits compacted to form these hard Limestones, which are more resistant to weathering than the surrounding Clays, and so have been left standing high and dry above the valley.

The underlying geology has determined not only the scenery, but also the vegetation which grows on its soil. The lighter soils of the Chalk hillsides and the Limestone ridges are better for arable cultivation than the sticky Clay, and these must have been heavily exploited for growing crops during later prehistory. In general subsequent centuries of farming have obliterated the archaeological evidence, but at the margins left untouched by the medieval plough, such as on Burderop Down below the hillfort at Barbury, a network of small field boundaries survives as earthworks to show just how far up the hillside the prehistoric arable farmer was prepared to go. The claylands provided other resources – woodland for building, fuel and pannage, clay for pottery, and, when cleared, grassland for pasturing cattle.

A glimpse of farming life in the Swindon landscape during the Iron Age was provided by archaeological discoveries made in 1976-7, when the Groundwell Farm industrial estate was being built. A sequence of four round wooden houses within an enclosure was excavated, together with granaries and other farm buildings. From pottery and animal bone it seemed that this was the working farm of a single family, and was in use from after 500 BC until before 200 BC. Their farming economy was mixed, and combined crop-growing (probably using oxen as draught animals) with the rearing of sheep and pigs. Pig bones were more numerous than on similar sites elsewhere, and this suggests that they were using woodland on the adjacent clays for pannage. The farmers seem to have been quite poor, since few metal implements were in use, and after the house and farmyard had been abandoned for several centuries the site was cleared and put down to arable, probably before AD 100. A reconstruction model of Groundwell Iron-Age farm is displayed in Swindon Museum.

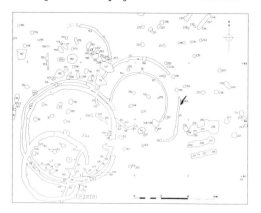

Plan of excavated Iron Age features at Groundwell Farm, including a sequence of four round houses (copyright WANHS)

Groundwell was probably typical of many small farms dotted around the Swindon landscape in later prehistory. They came and went, and some, such as a larger settlement excavated at Cleveland Farm, Ashton Keynes, continued as native communities during the centuries of Roman occupation. The Saxon place-name 'Walcot', which means something like 'the huts of the natives', may refer to one such settlement, and so this settlement must have survived beyond the end of the Roman period and still have been in use several centuries later ('Wal-' is related to our names Wales and Welsh, and was used by English-speaking Saxons to describe the native ethnic Celts whom they lived alongside or supplanted). By their activities, clearing woodland, manuring soil, making and consolidating tracks, building houses and marking out territories, the

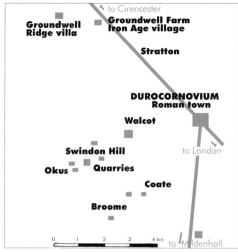

Summary map of Roman roads and settlements in the Swindon area

prehistoric and Roman farmers doubtless modified the landscape in ways which still affect modern Swindon; but how many of our modern roads and administrative boundaries owe their idiosyncrasies to such distant ancestors we shall probably never know.

Apart from the downland hillforts and field systems the oldest tangible pieces of human endeavour in the Swindon area are two Roman roads. Ermin Street, as part of the route from London to Cirencester is known, and another road which ran north from the Roman town at Mildenhall, near Marlborough, to meet it near Covingham, have both been superimposed over parts of their route by the A419 dual carriageway. The topography of Stratton St Margaret is patently dominated by the line of Ermin Street, and this link with Rome is a matter of local pride and folk etymology. 'You know what Stratton means, don't you?' I was once told by an elderly inhabitant, '—straight on!'. The name, which is Saxon, does indeed refer to Ermin Street, but not quite so blatantly: it means 'farm by the paved road'.

Few motorists today, belting round Swindon up the A419 from the Common Head roundabout, probably have time to ponder the fact that the bend in the road's direction from north to north-west is actually caused by the junction of Roman roads, nor that the name of the area to their left, Dorcan, is in fact a distant echo of the small town, *Durocornovium*, which Roman administrators established at that road junction. Part of this settlement was explored between 1966 and 1976, before much of it disappeared under the dual carriageway. The excavations suggested that a small community arrived here soon

The modern A419 looking north from the Wanborough Road bridge. To the right of Nythe Farm (centre left) is the site of the Roman town of *Durocornovium*. The Honda factory can be seen on the skyline.

Reconstruction (by the late Alison Borthwick) of the Roman pottery kilns at Shaw, West Swindon. The view includes a potter at work (right), firing a kiln (centre), and removing pots after firing (left) to load them on to a waggon for market. Living quarters, sheep and arable fields are in the distance

after the Roman road was built, perhaps as part of a military installation nearby. Later, in the second century a *mansio* was built north of the road junction. This was an official staging-post for Roman soldiers, messengers and other government staff – a kind of exclusive Macdonalds-cum-Travelodge for pass-holders only. Along the main road and in a grid of streets around the *mansio* a considerable town grew up. Undaunted by the low-lying terrain on the floodplain (their timber-framed houses were built on solid stone foundations) a community of craftsmen flourished in the third and fourth centuries AD, providing goods and services for the main road travellers, and a market for the surrounding countryside, including the whole of what has become the Swindon area.

The countryside around this 'proto-Swindon', *Durocornovium*, included not only the home-steads of small farmers, in the native Iron-Age mould, but also two other groups who arrived in the wake of Roman prosperity. During the second century potters colonized the claylands

and began to produce cooking pots, jars and other coarse pottery for the *Durocornovium* market. Evidence of their kilns was discovered in advance of the West Swindon development (one area has been named Kiln Park to commemorate their work) at various sites between Swindon and Purton, where not only the local clay could be exploited, but there was also ample woodland for fuel to fire the kilns. The industry, which probably supplied tiles for building as well as domestic pottery, had affinities with other production centres, at Gloucester and in Savernake Forest, but seems only to have flourished for two or three generations.

The other group to emerge around *Durocornovium*, as elsewhere, was a class of sophisticated farmer–landowners, who reorganized local agriculture on the basis of the villa

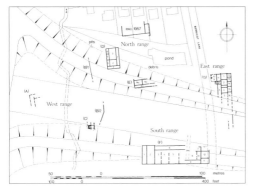

Plan of the Badbury Roman villa excavation hastily undertaken as the eastern slip roads for M4 junction 15 (also plotted) were under construction *(copyright WANHS)*

estate. Evidence of Roman villas, either the structures themselves or the trappings of luxury which accompanied them, have been found in various places around Swindon, including Purton, Stanton Fitzwarren, Chiseldon and elsewhere. One of the largest known villa complex in the area, and among the largest in England, lay next to the Roman road at Badbury. It was partially and very inadequately excavated during motorway construction between 1969 and 1971, and was found to have flourished almost throughout the Roman period. It included luxurious living apartments and working buildings spaced across an area of some two hectares, which is now largely beneath motorway junction 15 and its access roads.

But even this has been overshadowed in recent years by the discovery (first made in 1996 and still in 2005 the subject of archaeological excavation) of a complex of Roman buildings on Groundwell Ridge, during preliminary work for the Abbey Meads sector of Swindon's northern expansion. The site, on sloping ground facing south, is close to Blunsdon St Andrew, and less than a kilometre from Ermin Street. Extensive

Groundwell Ridge Roman site after the 2005 excavation campaign, showing its proximity to the North Swindon development, and the long views that the villa-owners would have enjoyed

and opulent underfloor-heated suites of rooms and bath-houses suggest a Roman villa on the largest and richest scale, but the complex also includes some kind of temple, or *nymphaeum*, built around the natural springs issuing from the hillside. Whether religious or residential, or both, the site was recognized as of such national as well as local significance that in 1999 it was bought back from the developer by Swindon Borough Council, so as to preserve the archaeology and create a public amenity – a far cry from the treatment meted out to Badbury villa thirty years earlier.

The owners of Groundwell, Badbury and the other villa-estates must have formed a powerful local aristocracy, and when the edifice of Roman rule, including their small town, crumbled in the fifth century, they did not immediately disappear. At Badbury, for instance, life under reduced circumstances appears to have contin-ued in the east range of buildings for a consider-able time; and at Groundwell later timber-framing has been found on top of Roman brickwork. Some of the landholdings associated with Roman villas may have remained as viable economic units through all the turmoil, only to reappear several hundred years later under Saxon landlords. We learn of the boundaries of such estates from surviving copies of the documents which conveyed them from one owner to another. Moredon, for example, now a Swindon suburb, first makes its appearance on the stage of history in 758, when the king of Wessex granted land there to Malmesbury Abbey. Nearly two centuries later, in 943, Moredon occurs in another charter, this time with a description of its boundaries.

Most of these boundaries can still be traced on the ground. They begin at a place called

Higford, 'the hay ford', which was probably close to where Northern Road now crosses the Rodbourne Stream. This stream, called *Hreod Burna*, 'the reedy brook', still lives up to its Saxon name in places, and the boundary ran west along it as far as its confluence with the River Ray (near the Purton Road/ Thamesdown Drive interesction). Next we can follow it north down the river to Tadpole Lane (by the station on the Swindon to Cricklade railway), then running east around the new Priory Vale development at North Swindon to Lady Lane; from there it was marked by what the charter calls 'an old ditch' as far as the foot of Penhill. After this it turned south, and tracing it among the houses of Haydon Wick and Pinehurst becomes more difficult. At some point it crossed the *Bradan Weg*, or 'wide way', which is presumably the modern Whitworth Road, and the name has been kept in use by the adjacent road, Broadway.

The confluence of the Rodbourne Stream with the River Ray

Moredon's charter, surveyed and written down over a millennium ago, defines an area uncannily similar to that of Swindon's northern expansion, begun during the twentieth century and now almost complete. And it is only one of several relating to places around Swindon which have survived. Others describe Purton, Badbury, Wanborough and part of Wroughton. Doubtless many more once existed which now are lost, setting out in meticulous detail the twists and turns of Swindon's ancient boundaries.

The Broadway, a modern street name with a very long history

To the historian the survivors are important for two reasons. In the first place they offer a kind of bridge between the territories of prehistory and the villa-owners on the one

The Saxon boundaries of an estate called Moredon

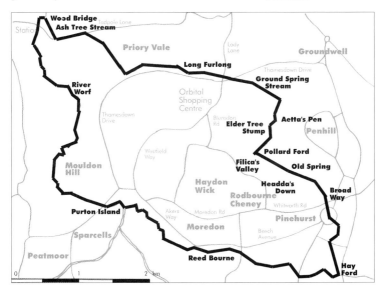

hand, and the later parishes and administrative units on the other, which have in turn shaped the development of towns like Swindon. In the second place they are repositories of Saxon place-names – often the direct ancestors of the modern names in daily use – which are themselves little capsules of information about Saxon landscape, people and settlements.

Familiar names which first occur in documents more than a thousand years ago include Groundwell ('the deep spring') and Chiseldon ('the gravel valley'). Three others – Moredon, Mannington and Ellendun – include the Saxon name element *dun*, which means 'hill' or 'high ground', whilst Lydiard and Penhill probably embody much older, Celtic, words for 'ridge' and 'promontory' respectively. At least ten other place-names around Swindon, including Swindon itself, are first recorded in Domesday Book in 1086, although they are likely by then to have been in use already for many years. Other names, not found until documents proliferate in the thirteenth century, were probably also first coined several centuries before. Most seem to be telling us about their position relative to the geological differences of Limestone, Chalk and Clay which we explored earlier. Thus a row of *dun* names is sprinkled along the Corallian ridge – Mouldon, Moredon, Haydon, Blunsdon, Kingsdown – whereas several clayland names suggest waterlogged or wooded conditions; they include Nythe ('land surrounded by water') and South Marston ('farm in the marsh') east of Swindon, and Shaw ('wood'), Sparcells ('wood for spears or spars') and Blagrove ('black thicket') to the west. Mannington (possibly 'Mehha's hill'), Chaddington ('Ceatta's hill') and Toothill ('the look-out hill') all seem to refer to minor eminences rising from the clay. The derivation of Swindon, 'the hill where pigs are kept', is well known, and refers of course to the Limestone ridge on which Old Town sits.

You may have noticed, when we explored the Saxon estate of Moredon, 'the hill of waste land', that the name of one prominent feature had already been used to denote the whole territory, almost all of North Swindon in fact, even though much of it lay alongside sluggish rivers and among sticky wood pasture, for which 'Moredon' was a quite inappropriate description. When in Domesday Book we find the name Swindon for the first time it had likewise come to be used for a considerable area, embracing in fact much of the large medieval parish, and consisting of five or six distinct landholdings.

The Penhill ridge, viewed from the south across Greenmeadow

Blunsdon 'Abbey', perched on high ground to the north of Swindon's recent expansion

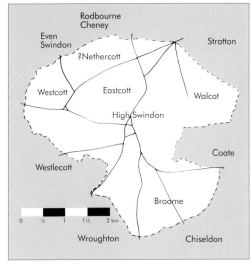

The ancient limits of Swindon parish, with its constituent and neighbouring estates

Thus separate names came into use for some of its constituent parts, such as Eastcott, Westcott and Nethercott ('the eastern, western and lower groups of cottages'), as well as the tautological Even Swindon. This literally means 'the hill of pigs on the flat ground', which would be nonsense, but of course what it really denotes is 'the flat portion of the Swindon estate'. By the thirteenth century, when Even Swindon is first recorded, we also find the expression 'High Swindon' in use to describe the area on the hill.

Around the time of Domesday Book, or a little before, the old Saxon estates became bound up with new territorial creations, the ecclesiastical parishes. The modern Swindon conurbation embraces most of three ancient parishes – Swindon itself, Rodbourne Cheney (which included Moredon and Haydon), and Stratton St Margaret – and has in recent years nibbled away at the clayland holdings of several others, such as Liddington, Wroughton, Blunsdon and the Lydiards. A parish might include several landholdings or manors – often the successors of Saxon estates – and the subsequent history and ownership of Swindon's Domesday manors have been meticulously traced. Their evolution need not concern us too much here, although we shall see further on how, even as late as the 1870s, manorial divisions had a crucial effect on determining where and when Swindon could expand. But two other topics on which manorial history impinges, medieval settlements and agriculture, do demand our attention at this point.

Evidence from archaeology, manorial records and medieval tax lists enables us to build up a picture of where people were living around Swindon and how they were supporting

The first portrait of a Swindonian. 'Here is Wadard', depicted on the Bayeux tapestry fighting at Hastings. In 1086 he was the tenant of Nethercott, one of Swindon's Domesday estates.

11

Blunsdon St Andrew church, marking the site of one of the medieval villages settled on high ground around Swindon

themselves. The larger and more prosperous communities were those to be found on the Chalk slopes or the Limestone ridge. Here, at places such as Chiseldon, Wanborough, Stratton and Blunsdon, villages were established which have continued to the present day. Several of these hillside villages, in addition to their fields of good arable land on chalky or sandy soil, possessed areas of Clay vale which they attempted to exploit as pasture grounds. The name-element *wic* is thought by most experts to denote a secondary settlement or farmstead concentrated on dairying, and so we find Liddington Wick (now beneath the Eldene estate), Haydon Wick (also now submerged beneath houses), Badbury Wick, and Wick Farm at West Swindon (formerly belonging to Lydiard Millicent) all down on the Clay below their parent communities. Swindon's own satellite hamlets on the claylands were probably little more than single farmsteads. In 1377 only 45 adult taxpayers lived in the combined territory of Eastcott, Westcott and Walcot, and another 27 in Even Swindon. These figures compare with 248 on Swindon Hill and 160 at Stratton St Margaret.

The fourteenth century was in general a time of retrenchment and shrinking population after many generations of growth. Among the poorer communities in the Swindon area some, such as Rodbourne Cheney and Even Swindon, managed to continue, while others, including Groundwell (with 11 taxpayers in 1377) and Moredon (with 16) came near to extinction. Mannington survived until the late fifteenth century, but was then deserted, and its corn-fields were converted to sheep pasture. Grassy mounds denoted the position of the villagers' dwellings, and corrugations of ridge and furrow

Westleaze deserted hamlet seen from the air, revealing the earthworks of property boundaries ranged along a street. The site lies south of Swindon between Okus and the motorway (*copyright Wiltshire CC*).

in the fields marked their acre strips of arable, until everything disappeared beneath the onslaught of West Swindon during the 1980s. Another community, which farmed part of Wroughton's claylands below Okus, is currently represented only by the earthworks and boundary banks of a former village street running from Westleaze to Westleaze Farm. Housing development in this area is planned to begin in 2006.

The parish of Swindon in the middle ages was divided between five manors, and each appears to have had its own farming regime. On the southern and eastern edges of the parish were the small manors of Broome and Walcot, and occupying Swindon Hill itself and its southern slope was the most productive of the estates, known as High or West Swindon. It included a very large arable field on the hilltop, which was later exploited also by the quarries, together with pasture grounds on the hillside. The two remaining manors, known as East Swindon and Nethercott (which included Eastcott and Westcott) consisted largely of clayland, but each extended some distance up Swindon Hill, on the north and east sides, to benefit from the lighter, more easily worked soils.

A Goddard estate map of part of Swindon made in 1763. Orientated with north to the right it depicts the town of (Old) Swindon at the top, and enclosed pasture fields over what are now the residential areas of Lawn and Walcot West (*WSRO X3/63*).

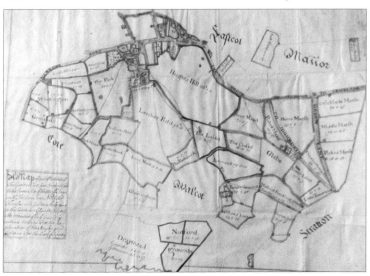

Both these poorer, sparsely populated manors attempted to grow crops during the middle ages in open fields on the unsympathetic clay soil of the valley; but during the seventeenth century they converted much of their land to enclosed pasture. The enclosure in 1657 of Eastcott manor (as Nethercott had by this time become known) was the subject of a long legal agreement between the various freeholders. This begins by reciting the various difficulties which the farmers were facing. It tells us that the grounds and premises, 'had for a long time past remained much impoverished and decayed by reason of the unaptness of the tillable grounds for corne and grain, which were more apt for grass and hay'. The disorders and inconveniences of the existing regime, it continues, 'could not heretofore be reformed by the reason of the disagreement and wilfulness of some of the inhabitants and occupiers of land there, and by reason of the diversities of tenures and estates, and the said grounds and premises so lying open and dispersed'. Accordingly the old common fields and meadows were divided up, and allotted in blocks to the various freeholders. This process of enclosure imprinted on the landscape many of the lines which, two centuries later, would constrain and be respected by the brand new streets and terraces of New Swindon.

The first Ordnance Survey map of the Swindon area, published in 1828, depicts a world far removed from that of fifty or a hundred years later. From the little foursquare hilltop town westwards to Lydiard, northwards to Blunsdon and eastwards to Wanborough stretched mile after mile of flat countryside, traversed by meandering streams and wandering lanes, and punctuated only by occasional isolated farms. Their names – Westcott, Penhill, Toothill, Walcot, Nythe – are entirely familiar to present-day Swindonians, but their surroundings are not. This older Swindon landscape has been almost completely forgotten, yet it underpins the entire structure and layout of the modern town and its suburbs.

The Swindon area mapped by the Ordnance Survey between 1811 and 1818, and published at a scale of 1 inch = 1 mile in 1828. The canals are a very recent addition to the landscape.

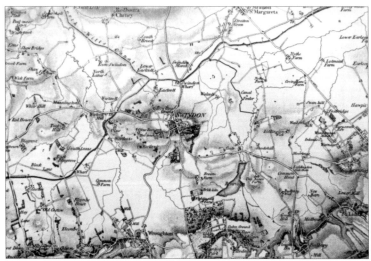

2 BUT A SMALL PLACE

'SWINDON IS A MARKET TOWN, placed on an eminence, which affords an extensive prospect over some parts of Gloucestershire and Berkshire. The pleasantness of its situation, combined with other circumstances, have induced many persons of independent fortune to fix their residence at Swindon; and their mansions contribute as much to ornament the town as their social intercourse may be said to animate and enliven it. To this may be attributed, perhaps, that liberality of mind which now appears to characterise the inhabitants of this little town.'

Square House, overlooking Old Swindon market place, one of the 'mansions' which John Britton may have had in mind

So wrote the topographer and antiquary John Britton, in part of his work about the 'beauties' of Wiltshire, which was published in 1825. By Swindon, of course, he meant Old Swindon – New Swindon did not then exist – and it is the evolution of settlement on Swindon Hill leading up to this plateau of Regency decorum which concerns us in the present chapter.

Stray finds of prehistoric artefacts, as well as archaeological work prior to new building, are developing a picture of intermittent human settlement on the hill from the time of nomadic mesolithic hunters and foragers through to the period of Roman colonization from *Durocornovium*. But prehistoric evidence here, generally in the form of flintwork, pits and burials, is really no more than might be expected on any tract of open, fertile, well drained and defensible land such as the hill during prehistory is presumed to have been.

Nor is it any surprise to find that astute Roman farmers and villa-owners also settled here – it would be more surprising if they did not. Over a century ago, in 1897, a local antiquary, Arthur Passmore, excavated part of what was probably a villa in the Okus area, and a few years later, in 1906, he also found evidence of a Roman building on the northern slope of the hill in what is now Queen's Park. Roman wells, ditches and building materials have subsequently been uncovered between Broome Manor and Coate. A fourth area of Roman activity on the hill, parts of which were excavated in 1975-6 and 1994, is perhaps the most important, because the site, a short distance due east of Old Swindon's market square around Dammas Lane, has yielded evidence from both earlier and later periods, as well as two phases of Roman buildings. The second Roman phase consisted of a rough stone-built structure, which could be dated from pottery and coins to the fourth century, not long before the breakdown of Roman rule. It replaced an earlier timber building on the site, and was in turn replaced by two small early Saxon huts.

These modest structures are perhaps the links in a chain which connects Roman *Durocornovium* with medieval Swindon and modern Old Town. We know that the community centred on *Durocornovium* was quarrying stone from Swindon Hill for some of its buildings, and there appears to have been a road leading up to the quarries from the Roman town. We have also seen that *Durocornovium's* low-lying position, dictated by the junction of the Roman roads, was far from ideal. Damp and flooding were clearly troubling the inhabitants, as some buildings there were raised above ground level, rather like granaries on staddle stones, and the problem may have been made worse by a deteriorating climate at the end of the Roman period. It has been suggested that the late-Roman and early-Saxon discoveries at Old Town perhaps represent a shift away from *Durocornovium* to a more viable site on the hill.

Not far away from where the Roman building had been buried a much larger Saxon hut, nearly nine metres long, was discovered. Its walls had been constructed of wattle and daub, and much of the daub, preserving the impression of the

Loomweights used to tension the warp threads during weaving, discovered by archaeological excavation where they had fallen during the fire which destroyed the Saxon weaving hut at Old Swindon

woven wattle structure, had survived the fire which ended the building's career during the middle-Saxon period. Beneath the daub were some of the hut's contents, including a shelf of pots and the remains of a loom and other weaving equipment. Like other Saxon huts discovered nearby its floor was below ground level, a characteristic of buildings of the sixth and seventh centuries. Another excavation carried out in 1977 behind Lloyd's Bank in Swindon High Street uncovered the same sequence of late-prehistoric and Roman settlement beneath a Saxon sunken hut, which had also been used for clothmaking.

Thus some kind of Saxon hamlet or village existed close to the centre of the later Swindon. The large weaving hut had later buildings superimposed upon it, which dated from the late-Saxon and early-medieval periods. But their alignment seemed to bear no relationship to the modern street plan. Indeed, more recent investigation detected a possible east–west street running across the line of the later High Street. It is probable, therefore, that between the middle-Saxon period and the twelfth or thirteenth century either there was a break in occupation or else a wholesale reorganisation of the settlement took place.

A likely context for any reorganisation of Swindon would have been an attempt to establish a market in about 1260, and so to turn the existing village into a small town. The archaeology so far described suggests that the earlier settlement may have been located to the east of the present High Street. Another clue to its position may be provided by the ruined church of Holy Rood next to the scant remains of the Goddard family's mansion now known as the Lawn, and close to the site of a mill. Although by all accounts an undistinguished building, the church was said to have incorporated a Norman

The ruins of Swindon's old parish church, Holy Rood, adjoining the Lawn, east of Old Swindon's market place

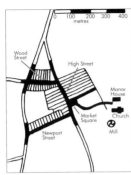

Conjectural medieval town plan of Old Swindon

column; this, together with a twelfth-century reference to a church at Swindon, suggests that it existed long before the market was set up. The mill is thought to have been the successor of one of the two at Swindon recorded in Domesday Book, and the Lawn is believed to occupy the site of its medieval predecessor. Their position therefore, some 300 metres east of Swindon High Street, tends to confirm the archaeological testimony.

If all these suppositions are correct then the present street layout of Old Town is likely to have been a planned addition tacked on to the western edge of an already existing village. Certainly the long, narrow strips known as burgage tenements running back from High Street and Wood Street suggest deliberate planning, and the expansionist mid-thirteenth century was exactly the right time for such a development. Similar urban extensions to existing villages occurred in many parts of England, and were common in Wiltshire between about 1210 and 1260. Sherston, Lacock and Market Lavington, to name but three, acquired markets and burgage tenure at this time.

This modern passage-way follows the edge of a medieval burgage plot running back at right angles from Wood Street (which can be seen through the gap in the distance)

Many so-called towns created in this way never developed into proper towns in the modern sense, and their medieval status could more accurately be described as that of urban villages. Indeed the three Wiltshire examples chosen have all been regarded for centuries just as large villages. In precisely the same way the medieval town of Swindon must not be overestimated.

The evidence for its urban career is remarkably slight. It seems not to have acquired a proper market charter during the middle ages and, were it not for a complaint by Marlborough tradesmen in 1274 that they had been suffering competition during the fifteen years past from an unofficial market in Swindon, we should have no idea when it began. There are, it is true, occasional references in medieval documents to a market and to burgages; there is by 1346 the appearance of the name Newport Street ('newport' means 'the new market'); and from 1289 Swindon was sometimes called 'Chipping' or 'Market Swindon'. An excavation in 1988 uncovered evidence of a possible boundary wall and wooden building in use in the fourteenth century on the corner of Devizes Road and Britannia Place; this is the first indication to be discovered that the town's built-up area extended so far westwards.

The earliest deed preserved among the archives of the Goddard family dates from 1436, and records the sale of a tenement in Newport Street *(WSRO 1461/1)*

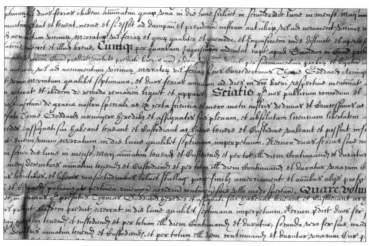

But the total absence of information about market trading and organization until the seventeenth century, the failure to secure a market charter until 1626, or to develop any kind of guild or corporate government – all are indications that medieval Swindon remained essentially a larger-than-average agricultural community, with perhaps a little quarrying as a sideline, and possibly a few more tradesmen and

Part of a document of 1626 granting to members of the Goddard family the right to hold a weekly market and two annual fairs at Swindon *(WSRO 1461/15)*

specialist craftsmen than its neighbours, but that its career as a town had scarcely begun.

Writing in the 1670s John Aubrey, the Wiltshire intellectual, attributed a rise in Swindon's fortunes during the previous thirty or so years to two factors, its market and its quarries. The market, he explained, had benefited from outbreaks of plague before, and probably after, the civil war. These disrupted normal marketing, and frightened cattle-dealers away from their usual centre at Highworth, some 10km to the north-east. Swindon, with its Monday market recently placed on a new and legitimate footing by the 1626 royal charter, appears to have taken and retained some of Highworth's trade. The civil war, too, was bad for Highworth. The town was garrisoned by royalist soldiers, who appear to have intimidated local graziers attending the market; in consequence they moved their business to Swindon.

Aubrey also claimed that the Purbeck Limestone, for which the town had become famous by the time that he was writing, was discovered in about 1640, only five feet below ground. Stone from Swindon Hill had been exploited, as we have seen, in Roman times, and doubtless supplied local needs during the middle ages. There is a reference to stone slates being taken from Swindon to Sevenhampton in 1301, and an old quarry is referred to in deeds from 1641. But it was during the seventeenth century that Swindon stone acquired a reputation, not only

Active and former quarries on Swindon Hill, mapped by the Ordnance Survey in 1886. Much of the area shown was landscaped to become the Town Gardens a few years later, in 1894.

for its smoothness and whiteness when used internally, but also for its resistance to damp. It was in demand during the rebuilding of London after the fire in 1666, and Aubrey implies that carriage was overland to Lechlade and then down the Thames. Certainly quarrymen begin to figure in Swindon manorial records from about 1670, both when they wished to purchase leases of lands for quarrying, and when they fell foul of authority for leaving excavations unfenced, to the danger of travellers.

Aubrey's impression of Swindon as a community on the increase during the seventeenth century is undoubtedly correct, and other sources of information help us to quantify its progress. During the eighty years prior to 1640 the new owners of High Swindon, the Goddard family, appear to have made only very modest progress. In 1563 their estate included 60 houses and 40 cottages; by 1640 this housing stock had increased by a mere 8, suggesting a rough total population on their manor at both dates of 400-450. During the 1640s there were at least 30 families on the other main Swindon manor, Eastcott, and probably a few others at Walcot and Broome, so we should perhaps add 150-200 to give an approximate total population of Swindon parish of 550-650. The principal Swindon manor more than two centuries earlier, in 1377, claimed 248 adult taxpayers, and this, after allowing for children and tax evaders, might also yield a total population of 400-450. Another 88 taxpayers (perhaps representing 150 inhabitants) lived elsewhere in the parish in 1377, suggesting a total in the range 550-600. These calculations, like most historical statistics, are fraught with uncertainty, but they do offer a superficial impression of stability or stagnation. One other figure, a claim in 1627 that 9 alehouses were too many for an adult population of fewer than 300, is perhaps an underestimate in order to strengthen an argument, but even if true would multiply up to a total population approaching 500, not far below our estimate.

Two further statistics bring the story down to Aubrey's old age. In 1676 a religious census returned 580 (adult) communicants in Swindon, which would suggest a total population of about 900. In 1697, the year of Aubrey's death, a list was made of the names of all Swindon's inhabitants. The manuscript was saved from burning by a Cirencester gentleman during the nineteenth century, and is now a little damaged, but it seems to yield a total of 795 names (791 and 808 are other people's computations). So we may be seeing a rise from 550-650 in 1640, to 800-900 by the end of the century, and Aubrey's

The Town Gardens, beautifully maintained, exhibit many changes of level, the result of quarrying, but also include works of public art

testimony appears quite credible. A further modest rise occurred during the eighteenth century, as by 1801 the population had almost reached 1,200.

But before we tackle the eighteenth century, the 1697 list deserves a second glance. Not only does it list everyone's names, but it also assigns an occupation to each householder. Thomas Goddard, who had been lord of the principal manor for nearly fifty years, heads the list, followed by members of the Vilett family, owners of the clayland manor of Eastcott, and Henry Thompson, vicar since 1663. We know, incidentally, from another source that the vicar was forever running into debt, and borrowing money from Goddard. Five other families are listed as having independent means, and there were fifteen yeoman families, accounting for some 7-8% of the total population.

The largest group, nearly one-quarter of the total, was made up of labourers and their families, but there were also significant numbers of textile workers – weavers, tailors and drapers – and masons (most of them quarrymen, no doubt), together accounting for about one-sixth of the workforce. The list includes most of the trades – such as bakers, coopers, saddlers, shoemakers, barbers, butchers and carpenters – which we might expect to find in any small town of the period, as well as one or two more exotic specialists. There is a tobacco cutter and a 'translator' (probably a cobbler who concentrated on renovating old shoes), a combmaker and a cheesefactor.

The existence of five or six inns and an alehouse implies that, although Swindon did not lie on a major road and so could not benefit much from passing trade, nevertheless the vigour of its market and quarrying industry was considerable. A survey in 1686 found that the town's inns could accommodate a total of 14 travellers and no fewer than 91 horses; perhaps they were geared to catering for long-distance waggoners with their teams.

The Goddard Arms in High Street, where an inn has stood since the seventeenth century

From a medieval urban village, therefore, Swindon graduated during the seventeenth century to the status of a small country town. It was a workaday place of tradesmen and labourers, and it had not yet developed the air of polite society which it exuded after 1800. It was still of less consequence than the neighbouring towns of Highworth and Wootton Bassett, and much less important than Cricklade and Marlborough. And it could still suffer put-downs. In 1731 a topographical writer sniffily remarked: 'It is so inconsiderable a place, that our histories take no notice of it'. As late as the 1790s a directory introduced Swindon as, 'but a small place, though the houses are well built, and of stone'.

Detail from the 1763 Goddard estate map, re-orientated so that north is at the top. The arrangement of streets is well shown, and the layout of the Lawn mansion within its grounds. Within the town it is likely that only properties in which the Goddard family had an interest are mapped.

Eighteenth-century Swindon, as depicted on maps of 1763 and 1773, consisted of three principal streets, forming three sides of a square. High Street continued southwards as Lower Town and northwards as Brookwell Hill or Brock Hill (present-day Cricklade Street), a much steeper descent than now and the scene of a fatal coaching accident. The market square, opening off High Street, included in its centre a small circular building, presumably of wood, which housed the pillory and stocks, and was used by traders as a shelter. It may have been, or have replaced, the market cross referred to in 1662; it was in poor condition in 1750, and was demolished in 1793 using chains and a team of horses.

Opposite the square, along the western side of High Street to the junction with Wood Street, a number of eighteenth-century and earlier

The Bell Hotel in High Street, purporting to date from 1515, with its massive bell

buildings have survived. The Bell Hotel retains work which may be of 1515, and other houses range in date from 1631 to the late-eighteenth century. At the northern end of High Street, facing Wood Street, is a building which was described by Sir John Betjeman as 'one of the most distinguished town houses in Wiltshire'. No.42 Cricklade Street was built in 1729, and became the home of the Vilett family, who owned Eastcott manor. Its architecture of local stone and brick marries the two foundations on

The Vilett town house, 42 Cricklade Street, built in 1729, and seen in 2005 prior to renovation

which Swindon is built, the limestone of Swindon Hill, and the clay of the vale. The present (2005) forlorn state of its once-proud façade, disused and unloved, provokes a sadness akin to that on seeing the state of the Mechanics' Institute (of which more anon).

Wood Street, which runs west from High Street, is first recorded by name in 1599, and is so called on a map of 1763. The name presumably refers, like its namesake in Wootton Bassett, to the fact that it leads towards Braydon Forest. But it also had two more colloquial names, Blacksmith's Street and Windmill Street, both because of premises adjoining it. It was remembered as a street of mean thatched cottages, and this poorer quarter continued down the hill along the lane known as Little London. Wood Street's present commercial character is largely Victorian, and results from the period when Old Swindon traders catered also for the needs of the burgeoning new railway town.

Victorian shops, hotels, banks and offices are ranged along the northern side of Wood Street, witness to the prosperity that Old Swindon enjoyed in the later nineteenth century

Newport Street, the third side of the square, runs at right angles from the southern end of High Street, and, like Wood Street, it had an alternative name. To old men in the nineteenth century it was always Bull Street, and was regarded as rather an eyesore. William Morris, whom we shall encounter in the next chapter, explained its derivation and character thus:

The *Bull* was a low, thatched, cottage looking building, very much like most of the other houses on the street. Indeed, if the houses on the street were not remarkable for their uniformity, it was owing to their all having been put up according to some rule of thumb . . . In a word, the architecture of the street may be described as that of the Squatters – of men who, by some means or other, became possessed of a bit of land, and built themselves a house thereon with such materials as came readiest to hand.

From this description it sounds very much as if Newport Street, after the planned medieval town had failed to develop, reverted to being a country lane, and was only built up again in the seventeenth century, by informal squatting when the town's population began to grow. Short Hedge, as the fourth side of the square of roads was known (now Devizes Road), remained in an undeveloped state until the nineteenth century.

Cottages (long demolished) in Newport Street, depicted on an old postcard

The bases of Swindon's economy, the market and the quarries, appear to have continued throughout the eighteenth century. A regular trade by stage waggon developed with London, carrying meat, cheese and other dairy products to the capital from its depot on the site of the later town hall or corn exchange. There are dark hints too about another, clandestine, trade, in smuggled spirits brought ashore along the south coast, and concealed in the cellars of Swindon houses.

The town's character was set, and local government controlled, by its forceful leading family, the Goddards. Despite repeated disputes with the vicar over tithes, which spilled over into litigation in 1777, the Goddards were no friends of nonconformity either. Pleydell Goddard in 1741 orchestrated a savage persecution against an itinerant evangelist, John Cennick, and his followers when he tried to preach in the town. According to Cennick's diary guns, halberds and a fire engine spraying ditchwater were all turned on them to intimidate and inflict injury, while Goddard, 'sat on horseback the whole time, laughing to see us so treated'. Such anatagonism was not uncommon, but it is eloquent testimony to the power wielded by the lords of the manor that nonconformity made virtually no impact in Swindon until after 1800, even though quarrymen elsewhere were generally staunch dissenters.

This ugly episode in 1741 was still remembered when John Britton was writing eighty years later, and he contrasted such prejudice with the liberality of the Swindonians he encountered. One indication of a small measure of enlightenment dawning on the town was a free school, established in Newport Street in 1764. It was administered by a trust, and its instigator and driving force (to give him his due) was Thomas Goddard, lord of the manor. The curriculum included the three 'R's and religious instruction according to Anglican principles; the teaching of science and foreign languages was not permitted.

A generation later, in 1804, an Independent chapel and dissenting academy opened, also in Newport Street. Thomas and James Strange, members of a leading Swindon family of bankers and tradesmen, sponsored the venture, and the first pastor/schoolmaster was a certain George Mantell, 'a fair scholar'. But his story, and that of his nephew, Gideon Mantell, belong to the next chapter.

The old order in Swindon. The Goddard house, later called The Lawn, stands beyond the old parish church, which is seen here in an engraving of 1850 shortly before it was abandoned

3 THE FIRST PUSH

GIDEON MANTELL spent the year 1804 in
Swindon, as his uncle's pupil at the new
dissenting academy in Newport Street. His home
was in Sussex, but he had studied under George
Mantell since 1801, and moved with him to
Swindon from Westbury, where he had been an
Independent pastor. George remained at
Swindon until his death in 1832, building up
the congregation and reputation of the Newport
Street chapel, and running his school for as
many as eighteen pupils at a time. Gideon
stayed in Swindon little more than a year,
before returning to Lewes to embark on a
medical career. But it was as a geologist and
palaeontologist that he made his name, and to
him is credited the discovery and first
description of several dinosaur species. In later
life, according to his diary, he paid four
nostalgic visits to the town, in 1827, 1832, 1841
and 1846. He died in 1852.

Mantell's life spanned the most important
period in Swindon's history. His schoolday
memories, of reading poetry in the shade of the
schoolhouse eaves, strolling in the 'Long Walk'
(part of the Lawn) with his adolescent first love
(who was a daughter of the prominent Strange
family), and collecting in the quarries the first
of the fossils which would shape his life – these
were Regency recollections of the genteel
country town to which John Britton has already
described to us. They are paralleled by the
school bills of a young lady, Miss Betty Wheeler,
who was being educated at Swindon between
1796 and 1800. Expenses included writing
books, dancing, shoes and gloves, a servant, a
trimmed bonnet, sash and umbrella, a 'filligree
caddy', and various items of haberdashery,
including 8s 8d (£0.43p, slightly more than a
labourer's weekly wage) spent on cord for her
stays.

Mantell's first return visit, shortly after the
former Miss Strange's death, was accomplished
by stagecoach as far as Marlborough, and then

George Mantell
was the first pastor
of the Independent
Chapel in Newport
Street, which was
built in 1803 and
opened in 1804

by post-chaise (a kind of private hire coach).
And his second visit, in 1832, was only a brief
stop while travelling by coach from Oxford to
Bristol. But in July 1841 he was able to travel
down from London, purely as a day's excursion.
He started at ten, he tells us, from the Great
Western Railroad at Paddington, and arrived at
the Swindon station at one, from where he
walked through the fields to the town. He
visited scenes of his youth, but spent most time
at the quarries collecting specimens. At six he
walked back through the fields to the railway
station, accompanied by a quarryman who
carried his heavy load of fossils, to catch the
seven o'clock train back to London. His last
nostalgic return, in 1846, was partly to meet up
with his son, a young civil engineer who was
working for Brunel on new railway lines in
Wiltshire.

Paradoxically, it was during Mantell's idyllic
year at Swindon, 1804, that the remote hilltop
town took a large step closer to the outside
world. Canals were an accompaniment to the
industrializing Midlands and North, and came
comparatively late to the South. Nevertheless
the linking of London and Bristol by water had
been proposed as early as the sixteenth century,
and various schemes to marry the Bristol Avon
and the Thames by canal were strenuously
advocated by John Aubrey in the seventeenth.
One of these was planned to extend from
Malmesbury on the Avon to Wootton Bassett,
heading presumably for the River Ray (a
tributary of the Thames) west of Swindon. But
as with most of Aubrey's ingenious projects, it
came to nothing.

Renewed interest during the 1790s led to
the construction of two canals across north
Wiltshire in order to achieve the union of Avon
and Thames, Bristol and London. The Kennet

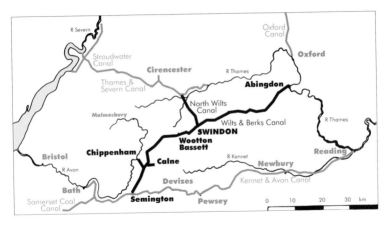

Map of the canals of
southern England

and Avon Canal took the southerly route,
through Devizes, the Vale of Pewsey and the
Kennet Valley. Branching from it, at Semington
near Melksham, the Wilts and Berks Canal struck
north and then east, through Dauntsey Vale to
Swindon and the Vale of White Horse.

From Chaddington near Wootton Bassett to
South Marston the canal maintained a level
course across the claylands north of Swindon
Hill. This stretch was the highest point, or
summit, of the navigation, and construction was
carried out from west to east between 1802 and
1805. A wharf was built below Swindon, and this
was in use by March 1804. The canal was
completed along its whole length in 1810, and
immediately plans were laid to connect it to
another canal, the Thames and Severn, which
ran through Stroud to Lechlade. The route of the

Coate Water, built as a
reservoir for the Wilts
& Berks Canal, is now
one of Swindon's most
popular outdoor
attractions

linking canal, which came to be known as the North Wilts, was decided in 1812. It left the Wilts and Berks near Eastcott (at the heart of modern-day Swindon) and ran north to meet the Thames and Severn at Latton. After much prevarication it was completed in 1819. Finally Coate Reservoir, to the east of Swindon, was built in 1821-2 in order to overcome chronic water shortages at the canal summit.

Looking back across more than fifty years of hindsight two local newspapermen, the old William Morris and the young Richard Jefferies, both saw the seeds of New Swindon in the arrival of the canal. It was 'the first push', according to Jefferies. Morris went further: 'It

was not only the greatest public work that had ever been undertaken in this part of the country, but the revolution it was to effect, and the impetus it was to give to trade, was simply marvellous.' More recent historians have tended to understate its importance, inexplicably in my view. For just as (for me) the key to decoding outer Swindon lies in the Roman roads, medieval farms and enclosure of the land beneath the modern suburbs, so the canal (more than the railway) unlocks the puzzles of central Swindon.

At the time the canal's effect was fourfold. First, and of greatest immediate interest to the residents of Swindon, it led to a spectacular reduction in the price of coal. Coal from the Somerset collieries (and after the North Wilts Canal was built from the Forest of Dean as well) was the main commodity carried along the canal, and local people came to rely on the cheap and plentiful supply to such an extent that, if in winter the water froze over and the

A restored section of the Wilts & Berks Canal at Rushy Platt, west of Kingshill

The canal, sketched when derelict in 1914, as seen from Bridge Street

barges were stopped, enterprising local farmers took waggons to the coalfield in order to make good the deficiency.

The second consequence of the canal was to stimulate the general trade of the area, by dispelling Swindon's rather aloof reputation, often repeated, as being a town which lay aside from main lines of communication. The canal opened up Swindon's agricultural hinterland, which in turn encouraged its market, and enabled it to increase its population in line with neighbouring towns and villages. Swindon's main producers of the period, however, its stone quarriers, appear not to have exploited to any great extent the possibility of cheaper and easier transport for their product which the canal offered. This may perhaps be attributable to the hostility of William Dunsford, the canal's superintendent from 1817 to 1839. Dunsford seems to have had extensive business interests 'on the side', which he tried to protect from competition, including a quarry producing Bath stone at Monkton Farleigh in west Wiltshire.

But the quarriers of Swindon did benefit from the canal in another way. During its construction (and long before Dunsford's arrival) they were called upon to supply large quantities of building and paving stone. Prodigious numbers of bricks, too, were made for the canal at temporary brickyards built close to the route. All this activity helped the local economy, which was further stimulated by the spending power of the itinerant navvies employed on building the canal. William Morris sarcastically commented on local people's supposed altruism regarding the navvies' welfare, 'especially so long as they had any money to spare, not of course for the purpose of getting it from them, but only to help them to take care of it, and see that it was not lost'(!).

But in addition to the effects which the canal had on Swindon at the time, there are two other reasons for emphasising its importance in the town's development. The first, which we shall consider shortly, is that its presence was one of the reasons expressed in 1840 for locating the railway works at Swindon. The second is the profound effect it has had on the layout of New Swindon.

This extract from a map of Wiltshire published in 1773 shows how empty the countryside north and west of Swindon was before the coming of the canal and railway

Prior to the nineteenth century, as we have seen, the boggy claylands north of Swindon Hill were very sparsely populated. Apart from Westcott and Eastcott Farms maps show nothing, and Britton reported that local people regarded one area, which they called 'quaving-gogs', as dangerous because of its deep quagmires. The building of the canal established a kind of base-line across the site of New Swindon which can still be clearly traced today. From the Cambria Bridge area it runs north-eastwards to become Canal Walk and the Parade, two of central Swindon's principal shopping streets; then its line is followed by Fleming Way to the 'Magic Roundabout', which is close to the site of Swindon Wharf. The railway, railway village, and Victorian housing in the Manchester Road area all owe their alignment to the canal. And because it was still very much in use while New Swindon developed and grew it acted as a barrier, so that anyone wishing to cross it had to use one of five bridges. These – Cambria Bridge, Milton Road Bridge, Golden Lion Bridge, Whale Bridge and Wharf Bridge – therefore functioned as benchmarks, dictating the northern ends of Commercial Road, Regent Street and Princes Street, and therefore influencing the entire layout of the Victorian town.

But these are matters to think about later, and must wait until after we have considered the circumstances and consequences of a certain

John Street bridge on the North Wilts Canal. The site, close to Fleming Way and the Parade was completely transformed, and is about to be redeveloped again.

The line of the canal under Milton Road bridge

famous picnic. Between 1801 and 1841 Swindon's population (excluding the recently arrived railway workers and itinerant navvies) increased by over 60%, from 1,198 to 1,952. Highworth, Wroughton and Wootton Bassett all returned increases of the same order. Swindon, therefore, was developing in line with its neighbours. Their increase was rather higher than Wiltshire as a whole (40%), but not quite as high as the United Kingdom average (almost 70%) over the same period. As Sir John Betjeman remarked: 'Anyone wishing to see what Swindon would have looked like . . . [if the railway works had not come] has only to look at Highworth, once the chief town of this corner of Wiltshire.'

There were a few buildings at Swindon Wharf, including a gentleman's villa, 'surpassing the second, and approaching the first class', according to William Cobbett in 1826 – the gentleman in question was William Dunsford, the canal's entrepreneurial superintendent. But apart from the wharf, Swindon's 60% growth to 1841 was absorbed within the existing town on the hill.

Evidence of the prosperity and expansion of these years may still be seen at Old Town. As a

Apsley House (Swindon Museum) in Bath Road, Old Town, the beginnings of Old Swindon's growth, after the canal but before the railway

schoolboy in 1804 Gideon Mantell drew a sketch map of Swindon, and this shows that Devizes Road (then known as Short Hedge or Horse Fair) was only built up at its northern end, where it joins Wood Street. Here six quarrymen's houses are depicted, three on the street, three set back along a lane. By 1818 Britannia Place had begun to be developed, and by 1841 there were twelve houses in Devizes Road itself. North of Wood Street, in Little London, was an area of poor houses, including a common lodging-house, and to the west developed the fashionable quarter of the town. Here, along Bath Road (then called The Sands) was built Apsley House,

Elegant porch on a brick town house in Bath Road, Old Town

which is now Swindon Museum, as well as the urbane brick terrace of town houses beyond, each with its cast-iron porch, and Prospect Place to the north, enjoying the open vista across the clay vale.

That vista was not to remain unaltered for long. In July 1833 a young engineer, Isambard Kingdom Brunel, was appointed in Bristol by a company which in the following month adopted the name 'Great Western Railway'. Its aim was to

Map of the Great Western and other early railways

link London, Bath and Bristol by rail. A route via Wootton Bassett and Wantage had been surveyed as early as 1824, and a similar line was recommended by Brunel in preference to the more southerly option, through the Vale of Pewsey. Parliamentary approval for the railway was secured in August 1835, and work began from both ends. This triggered residents of Bath's rival, Cheltenham, to petition for a connecting line from Swindon to Cheltenham, which was duly authorized in June 1836 as the Cheltenham and Great Western Union Railway. In December 1840 the railway from London reached Swindon, and a temporary station was built at Hay Lane, between Swindon and Wootton Bassett. In May 1841 the first leg of the Cheltenham line, as far as Cirencester, was completed, and in the following month Box Tunnel, the last and greatest obstacle on the line west to Bristol, was conquered, so that trains could begin to run between London and Bristol. Gideon Mantell, when he visited Swindon in July 1841 aboard the Bristol train, must therefore have been one of the first passengers. Swindon Junction Station, although in use from about May 1841, was not completed until July 1842, and the link with Cheltenham was finished in May 1845.

It is no use trying to appreciate these bald but momentous statements, unless we are prepared to dispel from our minds our hindsight of all that was to follow, and to put ourselves into Mantell's shoes, as he made his way across the fields back to the station with his fossils in 1841. The railways planned and built in the 1830s were the direct result of two factors: the success of the Liverpool and Manchester Railway (opened in 1830) in showing that steam locomotion between cities was a viable and profitable undertaking; and the availability of capital (and willingness of its owners) to speculate in similar projects. Of the hundred or so railway companies sanctioned up to 1840 most were concerned with relatively short distances; indeed by 1844 only 2,000 miles of track had been laid. The Great Western scheme was among the most ambitious of the early schemes, and was paralleled only by the Grand Junction (Liverpool to Birmingham) and the London and Birmingham, both opened in 1838. For shareholders, directors, contractors and employees alike – let alone passengers – the enterprise was fraught with risk and uncertainty.

For the Wiltshire countryman the possibility of a railway provoked a mixture of responses. Some, like the old farmer recalled in an anecdote by William Morris, refused to countenance the existence of such a thing. On being told about it, he took the news as, 'a most wicked and deliberate attempt on the part of an old friend to deceive and mislead him,' and could not believe that there would ever be a mode of travel to surpass the yellow post-chaise which he had seen with his own eyes. Others, including many landowners, greeted the prospect with hostility, regarding it as an intrusion on the privacy of their estates, and an unwelcome move towards social equality. In engineering their routes, railway companies repeatedly bent to the demands of landed interests. In Swindon the lord of the manor,

Homage to Brunel outside the shopping Plaza which bears his name

> ## SWINDON, WILTS.
> # A FREEHOLD ESTATE,
> *(Bounded on the south side by the line of the " Great Western Railway," and on the west side by the line of the projected " Cheltenham and Great Western Union Railway," and the North Wilts Canal ;)*
>
> FOR Peremptory SALE by PUBLIC AUCTION, by W. DORE, (by order of Trustees), at the BELL INN, in *Swindon*, on MONDAY the 18th day of April, 1836, precisely at four o'clock in the afternoon, under conditions ; consisting of three Inclosures of very useful and productive Meadow or Pasture LAND, containing together by admeasurement 21 A. 3 R. 15 P., lying in the tything of *Eastcott*, in the parish of Swindon, and now occupied by most respectable yearly tenants.
>
> This little Estate, independent of its locality, is desirable but when it is considered that both the above Railways will touch upon, or very near it, and that the important depot for the junction of the Cheltenham with the Great Western is not unlikely to be actually upon, and must be at all events very near this Property, its future value is incalculable. The speculator will rarely meet with such an opportunity of reaping profit at little risk. The Land Tax is redeemed, and it is divided into three Fields, and will be sold in two lots, as follows :
>
> | | A. | R. | P. |
> |---|---|---|---|
> | LOT 1.---Loppos Hill Grounds, with useful Stalls thereon, contains | 12 | 3 | 32 |
> | York's Upper Breach | 6 | 3 | 16 |
> | LOT 2.---The Three Acres, formerly part of Loppos Hill | 2 | 0 | 7 |
> | Total | 21 | 3 | 15 |
>
> Part of the Purchase Money, may remain on Mortgage, if required.
>
> For further information, apply to Messrs. CROWDY, Solicitors, Swindon.

A remarkably prescient newspaper advertisement, which appeared in April 1836, several weeks before the Cheltenham branch was sanctioned, and more than four years before the decision was taken to build the railway works at Swindon. Unfortunately someone has struck the advertisement through with a pen on this file copy of the newspaper, the *Devizes & Wiltshire Gazette*.

Ambrose Goddard, opposed a plan to build the line to the south of the canal, with a station at the foot of Drove Road, because it impinged on his parkland.

But such opposition was rarely fuelled by simple prejudice or inconvenience. Goddard, for example, as well as looking after his Swindon interests, was also from 1835 chairman of the Wilts and Berks Canal, whose fate was closely bound up with the new railway. Many local people watched the progress of the railway with interest, not as a potential threat but as a possible source of riches. In April 1836, before the Cheltenham branch was even ratified by Parliament, an advertisement appeared in a Wiltshire newspaper advertising fields at Eastcott for sale. Because of their proximity to the proposed railway lines, and the likelihood that a railway depot would be built near them – if not actually on them – it was claimed that they had an 'incalculable' future value. As it turned out, of course, the advertisement was no exaggeration, and Richard Jefferies recalled that one or two fortunes were made out of land which hitherto had been scarcely worth the trouble of attending to, and covered with furze.

If the prospect of becoming a railway junction was greeted with a mixture of prejudice, uncertainty and excited speculation,

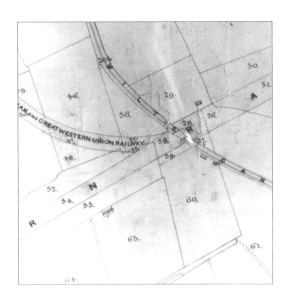

A small portion of Swindon's tithe map, drawn about 1840, which shows the relationship between the North Wilts Canal, the junction of the new railways, and the existing field boundaries which were about to be overrun by houses and the railway works

it was overshadowed in 1840 by an even more far-reaching proposal. Daniel Gooch, an ambitious engineer from Northumberland, was twenty years old when appointed Brunel's superintendent of locomotives in 1837. By 1840, with engines in service over much of the line and the prospect of completion to Bristol within months, Gooch was asked to recommend a site for a locomotive repair depot. There are hints in letters of the time of the company's, and Brunel's, indecision about this. A site near Bristol, or Reading, or Didcot, were all possibilities, and Brunel in 1840 was toying with developing Hay Lane, the line's temporary terminus near Wootton Bassett. But Gooch's recommendation was Swindon, and in a letter to Brunel on 13 September he set out some of his reasons.

Locomotives of the period were not considered capable of operating the entire distance from London to Bristol, and so a change would be necessary. Although Swindon was not halfway, it did lie at a transition, from the relatively flat and easy going tracks up the Thames Valley, to the shorter but more demanding descent through Box to Bath and Bristol. Swindon would be the convenient point at which to change to and from more powerful engines to tackle the western section. Furthermore, some kind of premises would in any case be necessary at Swindon, both to accommodate banking and pilot engines, and as a station to serve the junction with the Cheltenham line. Centralizing repairs there as well would be a sensible economy.

Gooch noted also that a suitable, level site was available in the angle formed by the junction of the two lines, and that the canal existed nearby, which would enable coal at a reasonable price to be brought to the depot. The principal drawback of Swindon, in Gooch's mind, was a poor water supply, but that in the last resort might be remedied by using the canal.

Soon after receiving the letter Gooch and Brunel visited the site, taking their lunch with them. The reality of the lunch is attested by Gooch's diary, and the story of the picnic, 'on the greensward which was then where the platform is now', was described in picturesque detail (including blossoming furze and frisking rabbits) by Richard Jefferies in an essay about Swindon published in 1875. Jefferies apparently was not aware of it when he wrote an earlier account of Swindon's origins in 1867, and in 1875 he wrongly attributes it to determining the line of the railway – this of course had been done much earlier, before Gooch worked for the Great Western. By 1913 the picnic legend ended with a stone, or even a sandwich, being thrown to decide upon the actual site of the railway works. Wittingly or unwittingly the foundation of plebeian New Swindon thereby paralleled that of its Wiltshire rival, patrician New Salisbury, whose site had been chosen (according to one version of the legend) by the flight of an arrow, shot by the bishop from the ramparts of Old Sarum Castle.

Sir Daniel Gooch

Whatever truth lies behind the primeval railway sandwich story, Brunel agreed with Gooch about his choice of Swindon, and the decision was endorsed by the Great Western Railway board of directors on 6 October 1840. But the apparently cogent operational reasons for the decision advanced by Gooch are by no means the whole story. Several recent authors have pointed out the impracticabilities of the scheme. In the first place the problem of water supply had not been adequately resolved. In fact poor water and sanitation were to blight the railway village and therefore the company's employees for many years. In the second place there was no obvious reason why the repair works should be cited alongside a depot for operational locomotives, especially on what was in effect a virgin site with no pool of skilled labour available. In the third place, while it was true that the canal at Swindon offered a cheap coal supply from areas not at the time accessible by railway, the same could be argued about Bristol, Bath or Chippenham, which were all much closer to the Somerset coalfield. Would not Bristol, where labour, water, housing and coal were all obtainable, have made better sense?

To explain Gooch's preference for Swindon there have been suggestions that he was in some sense implicated in land deals, or was being offered a commission on profits by speculators; and it has been observed that by 1852 he was able to spend £13,400 (a considerable fortune at Victorian prices) on buying Nythe Farm near Wanborough. Clearly he could have had financial interests in developing Swindon which he never declared, and it would be naive to think that no private consultations ever took place between Gooch and prominent Swindonians. It would be particularly interesting, for example, to know whether any deals were done with the Wilts and Berks Canal, and its chairman, Ambrose Goddard, which were not revealed to the respective companies' directors.

But there is probably no need to tarnish the reputation of Daniel Gooch in order to explain his advocacy of Swindon. Britain between 1837 and 1842 was in severe recession, and this not only applied the brakes to new railway schemes, but also forced companies which were already committed to building lines to seek economies wherever possible. The Great Western was in particular difficulty since building costs had far outstripped estimates. Now the site at Swindon for the locomotive repair works recommended by Gooch already belonged to a railway company, the Cheltenham and Great Western Union. It is not known how or why the company acquired it, but it was a valuable asset, since transferring it to the Great Western enabled the smaller company to extract certain operating concessions from the larger, and the larger to acquire the site for its works with virtually no expenditure at all.

The view from the gallery or footbridge at Swindon station, published in an 1852 guidebook, and showing broad gauge locomotives and track

The next problem which the impoverished Great Western board had to face was the cost of building workers' housing, and an appropriate station complex for the railway junction. Gooch's plan offered the solution. He had made out a persuasive case for Swindon as the point at which engines should be changed. The resulting delay to the train could best be occupied and disguised by providing passengers with refreshments. Such a concept was of course perfectly familiar to travellers brought up on stagecoaches, and it was already practised at Wolverton (now part of Milton Keynes), the equivalent point on the London and Birmingham Railway, where railway works had just been completed – alongside a canal, to boot. By February 1841, four months after Gooch's recommendation had been approved, the company was ready to announce that it had made a deal whereby a construction firm would build the station and the railway village at its own expense, in return for the exclusive franchise of the refreshment facility, and the rents of the workers' cottages. By choosing Swindon, therefore, the company obtained its station, its workers' housing and the site of its works for nothing.

Gideon Mantell paid a last visit to Swindon in 1846. By then the station, the works and much of the railway village had been built. But 1846 was another important year in Swindon's evolution. The works, as we have seen, were designed for the repair of existing locomotives. In 1846, for the first time, new locomotives were manufactured at the works, and Swindon's revolution was fulfilled.

4 A GOD OF STEAM

LIKE CREWE, Swindon during the 1840s rose from obscurity to become a household name. 'Swindon, all-important Swindon,' boasted a promotional guidebook to the Great Western Railway in 1852; 'who that knows aught of railways, or railway travelling, has not heard of Swindon's world-wide reputation, as well for the vastness of its workshops and engine depot, as for the admirable and splendid accommodation that it furnishes to the way-worn traveller?' A page of mouthwatering grandiloquence follows about the station refreshment rooms, ending with the opinion that, 'here we have a close approximation to perfection, accompanied, too, with undeviating civility, and a moderate tariff'.

The guidebook writer, replete no doubt with free helpings of the banbury-cakes and sherry-cobler which he eulogized, was spot on in his opinion that Swindon's reputation was made by its refreshment rooms. But it was not the reputation that Swindon might have wished. Despite the architecturally impressive

An idealized portrayal of the refreshment rooms for first-class passengers at Swindon station in 1852

The station buildings at Swindon depicted by George Measom in his 1852 guide to the GWR. Later editions of the guidebook tended to gloss over Swindon.

surroundings, travellers did not share his enthusiasm, either about the quality or price of the 'choice refections'; indeed the nickname 'Swindleum' began to be applied to the establishment. Brunel himself was among the first to complain, within months of its opening. His letter to the caterer has often been quoted, in which he denies calling the coffee 'inferior' – he had actually called it 'bad roasted corn'. Older travellers perhaps recalled to mind the similar 'rip-off' mentality of innkeepers during the coaching era. Unfortunately for Swindon, it was the enforced refreshment stop and the exorbitant prices that travellers first encountered, and that stuck in their memories, rather than the other themes with which the present chapter is concerned: the locomotive works, the railway village, and the effect of the new town on the old. So we had better dispose of this embarrassing topic first.

Swindon Junction Station, with its elaborate refreshment rooms and hotel, was built in 1841-2 by J D and C Rigby, a London firm of builders, at their own expense, and its architecture survived largely unscathed until redevelopment of the site began in July 1972. The buildings comprised two three-storey blocks with basements, linked by a footbridge which straddled the main line. The ornate refreshment rooms, for first and second class passengers (segregated) only, were at ground floor level, with kitchens below and hotel above.

As part of the deal Rigbys were leased the sole catering franchise at Swindon for 99 years on a peppercorn rent. In the early days a change of engine at Swindon was an operational necessity, as we have seen, and so the company agreed that all trains would make a stop of about ten minutes at Swindon. This would be the only refreshment stop between London and Bristol. Rigbys sublet and eventually sold this franchise, but the ten-minute stop was rigorously enforced by the caterer long after the change of engine was no longer necessary. This

The lower part of this western range of the NMRC building is part of the original 1843 GWR general offices.

The engine house in 1846, where routine maintenance to locomotives was carried out. The house could accommodate 36 engines, like horses in stables.

exasperating delay, along with the exorbitant prices charged for mediocre food, continued to irritate the company and its passengers until 1895, when the GWR paid the princely sum of £100,000 to buy out the franchise-holder. By then, of course, the Swindon refreshment rooms, and by association the town itself, had become the butt of music-hall humour – the ignominy of much maligned Swindon had begun.

The locomotive depot and repair works, sanctioned by the board in October 1840, were begun in 1841 and completed before the end of 1842, for regular use from January 1843. Brunel was responsible for designing them to Gooch's requirements (the job was probably delegated to an assistant, T.H. Bertram), and Rigbys were employed as contractors. At the heart of the original works were two large sheds, abutting to form a T-shape. The cross-piece of the T, parallel with the Bristol line to its south, was the engine shed; adjoining it on its northern side was the repair shop. Other necessary buildings, including the smiths' shops, wagon shops, the erecting shop and the offices, were arranged around this T, rather like quadrangles around an Oxford college. Some elements of this original design, though much modified, have survived, notably part of the English Heritage building, one wall of STEAM, and Churchward House. The master of the establishment, under Daniel Gooch, was a Scotsman, Archibald Sturrock. Like Gooch he was in his early twenties, and the two men had become friends before either joined the GWR. He stayed with the company, as works superintendent, until 1850, then was employed for sixteen years by the Great Northern Railway. In 1866, aged 50, he retired, but did not die until New Year's Day, 1909, 42 years later.

The works quickly progressed from repairing to manufacturing rolling stock, including carriages and wagons, and (a revolutionary step for an operating company in those days) in February 1846 the first locomotive, named *Premier*, was produced. The GWR, locked in controversy over the merits of the broad gauge compared with its rivals' narrow (now standard) gauge, was eager to show its superiority, and in January 1846 Gooch was instructed to build, 'a colossal locomotive working with all speed'. Thirteen weeks later the engine, *Great Western*, was running, and showed that it was capable of hauling passenger trains over long distances at an average speed of nearly 60 mph. Twenty-eight more express passenger locomotives were built at Swindon between 1846 and 1851, as well as many smaller goods engines. They established the works at the forefront of railway technology, and its reputation was underscored in 1851 when one of its progeny, *Lord of the Isles*, was exhibited at the Great Exhibition.

But reputation was not enough. Swindon began its manufacturing career during the railway mania of 1844-7, when companies such as the GWR over-reached themselves with ambitious plans for expansion. Following the

Part of the remarkably detailed panorama of New Swindon painted by Edward Snell in 1849, showing the railway works

The Lord of the Isles, a famous product of the Swindon workshops, which was displayed at the 1851 Great Exhibition. To have its photograph taken it stands outside St Mark's church.

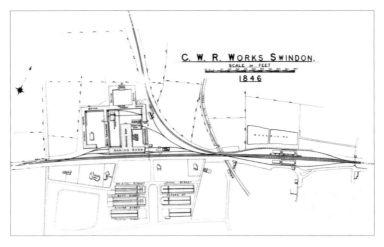

Plan of the railway works in 1846. Notice that the railway village is only partially built, and that the boundaries of the new development correspond with those of the fields shown on the tithe map of about 1840 (see page 38 above).

repeal of the Corn Laws in 1846 and the influx of cheap imported grain the stock market collapsed in 1847. The GWR was in serious financial trouble and retrenched its operations. At Swindon the workforce had risen from about 400 in 1843 to 1,800 by 1847, after which it was savagely cut to 600. Several senior officers, including Sturrock, resigned rather than face a cut in salary. Recovery was gradual, but at Swindon it was helped by a new dimension during the 1850s, as the GWR acquired Midland companies operating narrow (standard) gauge lines, and required locomotives and rolling stock for them.

Railway engineering in general, and Swindon works in particular, was the high technology of the 1840s. It demanded a workforce quite different from either the uncouth navvies who built the lines, or the pastoral farmhands who inhabited the neighbouring north Wiltshire countryside. Skilled engineers and fabricators, like oilfield workers in the North Sea during the 1980s, and computer programmers during the 1990s, commanded a high premium, and travelled to Swindon from all over the country to work hard for high wages. Analysis of the 1851 census for New Swindon shows that nearly 15% of the population originated in Scotland or Northern England, and nearly 10% in London and the South-East; the equivalent proportions in Old Swindon were 1% and 4%. A study of the careers of many New Swindon pioneers has shown that some were 'headhunted' by Gooch and Sturrock from places where they had worked previously – Dundee, the North-East and south Lancashire. There seems even to have been a kind of recruitment agency operating for Gooch in Liverpool.

It was clear to the GWR board when they decided to site the works at Swindon that accommodation for their employees would have to be provided. We have already described the deal whereby Rigbys built at their own expense cottages for the workforce on land which the GWR had purchased, in return for fixed rents from the occupants. It is time now to examine the outcome of this arrangement.

The development of New Swindon as a community may be compared with two other English towns which owed their origins to railway works on 'green field' sites, Crewe in Cheshire, and Wolverton in Buckinghamshire, now part of Milton Keynes. Wolverton's railway works were begun by the London and Birmingham Railway in 1838 and, like Swindon's, were sited at the point on the line where a change of engine was necessary and a canal was at hand. The population grew from 417 in 1831 to 2,070 in 1851, and the new town was built as a grid of 242 red-brick terraced houses, with a church, a school and several pubs. That Wolverton was in the GWR directors' minds when they sanctioned the development at Swindon is clear from their report, in which the place is specifically mentioned. Crewe, the creation of the Grand Junction Railway, was exactly contemporary with Swindon, since its railway works were begun in 1841. Early housing, some with Gothic detailing, included a range of accommodation reflecting the status of its occupants within the works.

The southern portion of Edward Snell's 1849 panorama of New Swindon. The regularity of the railway village, and the open area at its centre, are clearly seen, as well as St Mark's church in the foreground.

At Swindon two blocks of four parallel streets were laid out and built up with terraces of cottages, largely between 1842 and 1846. The streets took their names from destinations of the trains which passed nearby – Bristol, Bath, Exeter and Taunton comprised the western block, London, Oxford, Reading and Faringdon the eastern block. The western block was built up quickly, mostly in 1842 and 1843, but the eastern block took much longer to complete –

Restored cottages in the railway village

not until 1855, in fact. The terraces are of two-storey cottages, generally with one or two bedrooms, and built of local Swindon stone with some dressings (quoining and around windows and doors) of Oolitic Limestone, possibly won during the building of the cuttings leading into Box Tunnel. Between the two blocks of terraces, running north towards the works entrance, was a wide boulevard-like area originally called High Street, and by 1848 larger houses had been erected facing it at the end of each terrace. The Mechanics' Institution and Medical Fund Hospital were subsequently built on this open area, and it was renamed Emlyn Square after Viscount Emlyn, a GWR chairman. Most of the railway village, as this estate is known, was purchased by the local authority in 1966, and renovated between 1969 and 1980. One cottage (which is, however, not typical of the estate as a whole, since it is later and larger than most) was opened as a museum in 1980, and was furnished and decorated to appear as it might have done in about 1900. It is not currently (2005) open to the public.

Since 1945, and perhaps before, a tradition has grown up in Swindon that the railway village was designed by the eminent Victorian architect and architectural writer, Sir Matthew Digby Wyatt. It is true that between 1852 and 1854 he collaborated with Brunel on the design of Paddington Station, and so had a connection with the GWR. But that was later. In 1841, when work began on the railway village, he was barely twenty, and was saving to go on the Grand Tour by working in a drawing office, and also undertaking small architectural commissions – a school in Wales, two houses near Dublin and a

London factory building. While it is possible that Rigby's sought his help for Swindon, no connection with the project is mentioned by his biographers or appears in his list of works. Another objection to the theory of his involvement is that, although the railway village has a unified appearance, there are significant differences of architectural detail between the terraces, as if modifications were made as the building work progressed. Wyatt spent two years, 1844-6, touring on the continent, and so could not have been directly involved with the project as it took shape.

The railway village repays study nevertheless. The problem of housing large working communities close to new industrial complexes was not new in the 1840s. It had been faced by colliery and mill owners in the Midlands and North for several decades, as the industrial revolution invaded remote and unpopulated areas. Some of the resulting employer housing was of very poor quality, but by the 1830s two arguments had emerged for providing reasonably good living conditions for the workforce – that they helped to recruit suitable and desirable employees, and that they enhanced productivity by reducing illness and improving morale. What had not yet emerged by 1840 were the conclusions of inquiries linking poor sanitation and water supply with disease, which led to the passing of public health legislation in 1848. Nor was the era of

One of the back alleys which run behind the railway village cottages. Rudimentary drainage ran under the alleys from privies in the back yards on either sides, and was a source of squalor and ill-health in the early days.

philanthropic housing schemes, initiated by
benevolent societies and conscientious
employers, yet under way – although it was just
beginning, and a few notable experiments had
been tried.

It was against this background that the
railway village emerged. Despite the aura of
paternalism which the company later managed
to convey, the GWR in the 1840s was not, and
could not afford to be, a philanthropic
organization. It could not justify to its
shareholders what might be seen as unnecessary
expenditure on moral or religious grounds. In
fact it rather side-stepped responsibility for
housing its workers through its deal with
Rigby's. And Rigby's, driven no doubt by normal
commercial considerations of the rate of return
on their investment, built to a standard which
they considered would warrant the rent which
skilled engineering workers could be expected to
pay. If that standard was quite high, it was
because Rigby's had saved money by not having
had to purchase the site, there was a bountiful
supply of good building stone, and the intended
occupants were comparatively well paid. The
main drawback, which was exacerbated by early
overcrowding in the village, was the old bugbear
which Gooch had identified in his original
report, the problem of water supply and
drainage.

Edward Snell, who became Assistant Works
Manager in about 1849, and who painted the
famous panorama of New Swindon in that year,
was one of the first inhabitants of the railway
village, arriving at the end of February 1843.
Soon afterwards he wrote in his diary:

> For my part I hate it and haven't been well
> since I've been here . . . A precious place it is
> at present, not a knocker or a scraper in the
> whole place. Most of the houses very damp and
> containing only two rooms . . . Not a drop of
> water to be had but what comes from the
> tenders or out of ditches and what little we do
> get is as thick as mud – not fit for a jackass to
> drink. The Company make the men pay most
> extortionate rents for these bits of huts, too –
> 3s. 6d. for a single and 7s. for a double cottage
> and won't allow any of the men in their employ
> to sell anything whatever. We have a couple of
> Doctors' Shops which are pretty frequently
> visited, a Great Western Sick Club, a school . . .
> and a chapel.

Snell's experience confirms the impression of
squalid, overcrowded and unhealthy conditions
given by other sources. Smallpox, typhus and
cholera occurred there during the first decade.

Admittedly living standards may have seemed worse to Snell – he was born in Barnstaple and apprenticed in Bath – than to other newcomers accustomed to urban overcrowding in Sunderland or Liverpool. His mention of the various social amenities already available in New Swindon is remarkable, because, written in 1843, it antedates the usually accepted date for any of them. He cannot have made them up, however, and the existence of the chapel is confirmed by a document preserved at Gloucester. This records that in June 1843 a group of Methodists were holding services in a room next to the Golden Lion Inn near the Swindon Railroad Station; they were under the leadership of a Wesleyan minister from Marlborough with a wonderfully Old Testament name, Zephaniah Job.

An engraving of St Mark's church, made at the time of its opening in 1845

During the 1840s and 1850s the amenities mentioned by Snell, and several others, became established in their own buildings. They were supported by the company in various ways, and some acquired GWR as a handle to their names, but in general they did not originate with the company and were not officially funded. Thus the GWR church (St Mark's) and the GWR school next to it resulted from a bequest in 1842 by C.H. Gibbs, a director, and were built on land donated by Colonel Vilett. St Mark's Church, 'all spikes and prickles outside', was completed in 1845 on land immediately west of the railway village. In an essay published in 1952 Sir John Betjeman paid the church, and the community which worshipped there, a unique compliment: 'One cannot call it a convenient site . . . But it is a strong church and though it is not much to look at, it is for me the most loved church in England.' The school opened during the same year, and was soon suffering the same overcrowding as the rest of the village. In 1847 it had 168 pupils and only two teachers. The GWR park, abutting the school and church, was given by Colonel Vilett to the company as a public amenity in 1844.

The GWR Mechanics' Institute, shut up and derelict in 2005

The two most prestigious organizations stemming from the early years of the railway village were the mechanics' institute and the medical fund. Gooch claimed to have started the institute in January 1844, in response to complaints from the

The reading room within the Mechanics' Institute in its heyday, sketched in 1914

neighbouring gentry about drunkenness and disorder: 'I got together those of the workmen whose moral character was superior to their fellows and formed them into a Workmen's Institute.' In fact its genesis probably lay in an informal lending library begun by employees a few months' earlier. Under the name 'New Swindon Mechanics' Institution' the organization rapidly grew, and provided not only evening classes and the library, but also entertainments of various kinds, including theatre, concerts and dances. One event organized by the institute in 1849, a free excursion to Oxford, proved so successful that an annual 'Trip' by train developed as a kind of works' outing, and ultimately as the annual holiday for employees and their families. In 1855 the mechanics' institute moved into purpose-built premises in the centre of the railway village, which had been built by a company set up for the purpose and chaired by the works superintendent. An octagonal market hall adjoined the institute building. The mechanics' institute library continued to

The octagonal covered market, which was attached to the Mechanics' Institute, and was demolished around 1891 when the institute was extended

function as a public library for Swindon until the second world war.

The GWR Medical Fund Society traced its origins to the period of distress caused by the lay-offs and short-time working introduced in 1847. It appears to have been an employee-led initiative to create a fund which would pay the surgeon to attend both working and laid-off staff and their families. To pay for the scheme every employed man would pay a small weekly subscription; but Gooch successfully sought company blessing, and assistance in the form of a rent-free house in the railway village for the surgeon, and an annual stipend for the surgeon to cover attendance to accidents at work. A society was formed to administer the fund, and this eventually grew to such proportions that in 1871 it built and administered its own hospital next to the mechanics' institute.

One other prominent establishment of the period was intended to solve the overcrowding problem. This was a lodging-house for single men, which Richard Jefferies claimed could accommodate 500, and was 'a vast place, with innumerable rooms and corridors'. It was begun in 1849 and completed in 1852, but the austere pile was immediately unpopular, and was nicknamed the 'Barracks'. Little occupied, it was

The unpopular 'Barracks', or hostel for single workers. In 1869 it reopened as a Methodist chapel, and from 1962 until 2000 it housed the railway museum.

later turned into flats for an influx of Welsh workers, then sold to become a chapel, and from 1962 until replaced by STEAM in 2000 was employed to house the railway museum.

In 1850, and for many years to follow, there was open countryside stretching down the hillside which separated old, respectable Swindon from this alien aberration of the railway revolution. How strange, how disconcerting, how fascinating it all must have seemed to the Wiltshire countryman – the unintelligible accents of the newcomers, the fearsome power unleashed by the engines, the

The Wilts & Dorset bank of 1884 on the corner of Wood Street and Cricklade Street. Businesses in Old Town prospered as New Swindon's population grew.

massive buildings, spanking new. That intervening mile of grass and agriculture was doubtless a comfort to many in Old Swindon, but it was not far enough to allow the town to vegetate in some xenophobic cocoon. In fact the effect on it of New Swindon was profound. A government inspector, called in to examine the town's public health, reported in 1850 that: 'The old town of Swindon has materially increased in numbers and wealth since the completion of the railway. The houses built have been of a superior class; and the tenants, being more or less connected with the railway, are a well-behaved and intelligent class of persons.'

So this was one consequence of the railway works, that some of the better-paid employees found their way up the hill and made their homes in Old Swindon. But many more of the newcomers, wives and young children especially, were familiar with the trek across the fields for another reason. In the early years of the railway village there were few shops, and most food and provisions consumed in New Swindon had to be purchased in the old town, and carried back down Eastcott Hill, which was then a narrow field path. 'Those were rosy days for Old Swindon shopkeepers and publicans', recalled an old man who had grown up at Prospect in the 1860s. The railway workers were paid fortnightly, on alternate Fridays, and then large sums of money changed hands in Old Town.

There is no doubt that wealth created in the railway works stimulated Old Swindon's economy. But even without that the town seems

Bath Terrace, early Victorian shops at the junction of Bath Road and Devizes Road. (The girls were on a work-experience mission interviewing and photographing passers-by for the *Evening Advertiser*. I seem to have got my own back!)

to have been doing well during the 1840s. A directory description published in 1848 was particularly up-beat about (Old) Swindon's progress. New streets were being laid out, the general appearance of the town was improving, and the shops now equalled those of Bath and Cheltenham. A large assembly room had recently been added to the Goddard Arms, and there were plans to build a town hall and market house. The old church was too small for the growing population, and so there were proposals to replace it with a new one. The cattle market was making a great name for itself, and the flourishing quarries were major employers. All in all, 'Swindon may now, perhaps, be said to be one of the most flourishing and promising towns in Wiltshire'.

The permanent (as opposed to transient) population of Old Swindon in 1841 cannot be accurately deduced from the census, but was probably of the order of 1,800–1,850. In 1851 it was 2,294, which represented a rise of about 25%. To accommodate the extra families new houses were built and new streets laid out. They were given patriotic names – Britannia Place, Victoria Road, Albert Street, Union Row – and most of them have survived to the present day. But for all its pretensions the expanding town

Old Swindon's classical town hall of 1852, and Italianate tower added to the adjoining corn exchange in 1862. The town hall's ground floor was intended as a market but never so used. After careers as skating rink, cinema, dance and bingo hall, this once proud edifice is now in a deplorable state.

had problems. Sanitation was poor, water sources were becoming polluted, and disease was rife. The inspector called in to report in 1850 discovered that life expectancy had reduced from over 36 years in the whole parish during the 1820s to 29 years in Old Town in the 1840s. He recommended that a sewerage and water supply system be provided for the town, and that a local board be set up to oversee it.

However different Old and New Swindon might have appeared, they could not for long escape the fundamental problem common to them both – that the provision of services was not keeping pace with the rising population. These and other growing pains were to continue for another fifty years, until Old and New disappeared, and Swindon became simply Swindon again.

Christ Church, Old Town, built in 1851 to replace the old parish church (Holy Rood) at the Lawn

5 BRICK-BUILT BREEDING BOXES

THE NEXT CLUE to decoding Swindon involves statistics. Swindon in 1851 had a population of 4,879, almost equally divided between the old and new towns. A half-century later, in 1901, the census returned a total of 45,006, and no longer distinguished between old and new. This was because in the previous year the two communities had united to become a municipal borough. During the same half-century the population of England and Wales rose by 81%; but that of Wiltshire rose by only 8%, and if Swindon is left out of the reckoning, the rest of Wiltshire's population actually declined by 8%. Swindon meanwhile increased by nothing short of 822%. The goal of the present chapter is to account for this astounding jump (far greater than anything achieved since 1901), and to examine its impact on the Swindon which we see around us.

We left the railway works in trouble at the end of the 1840s, with its workforce slashed to 600. By 1900 the payroll had risen by leaps and bounds to about 11,500. Four interrelated factors were responsible not only for the leaps and bounds, but also for intervening episodes of setback and disappointment. First were periods of expansion and retrenchment in the national economy of Victorian England. Second were technical improvements and new legislation affecting railways. Third were the fortunes of the Great Western Railway, as it built new lines and took over competitors, but also teetered towards bankruptcy. And fourth were decisions taken by the company's directors to centralize its engineering activities at Swindon.

Recovery after the desperate days of 1847-9 was accomplished at first by diversifying to build components for bridges and other civil engineering works. Later, in 1854, the GWR purchased rival companies in the Midlands which used the narrow, or standard, gauge. This resulted in the need for new locomotives and rolling stock, which Swindon began to produce in 1855. Then in 1860-1 Daniel Gooch persuaded his board to build a rolling mill at the works, which would produce better and cheaper iron rails than they could obtain from outside contractors, and would also be a way of recycling scrap iron from Swindon's other manufacturing processes. During another railway boom in the 1860s the GWR, saddled with its broad gauge, was beleagured by competing railways. They tried to encroach on its territory with plans for standard gauge lines, and large sums were spent on legal actions opposing them, as well as in proposing new lines of its own. In 1866 the company had overreached itself and was almost bankrupt; it was only through skilful negotiation with its creditors that Daniel Gooch, newly appointed chairman, drew the GWR back from the abyss.

This cloud of financial ruin had a silver lining for Swindon. The company had since 1865 been thinking about establishing new carriage works at Oxford. Gooch now persuaded his board that Swindon would be a cheaper alternative, because company-owned land was already available, in the area between the railway village and the main Bristol line. Here, abutting Bristol Street and London Street, the carriage works were begun in 1868, and it is their fortress-like façade of stone and glass, some 350m long, which for over a century separated living Swindon from working Swindon. A decade of expansion and prosperity for Swindon works followed, stimulated largely by the gradual changeover from broad to standard gauge. Orders for new locomotives and rolling stock to meet the change kept Swindon busy, and justified wholesale modernization of the factory.

The boom ended in 1877/8, and no further expansion took place at the works until 1887.

The south wall of the carriage works, which since 1868 has divided the town from the works. The tunnel entrance may be seen at pavement level below the gable

Nationally these were years of severe depression, and one consequence was a reduction in demand for rail traffic. The GWR found itself over-resourced, and imposed a freeze on orders for new stock. Swindon suffered less than some other establishments, however, as the company chose to centralize work on its largest plant, and by judicious accounting, routine repairs, and work on new safety modifications, the railway works managed to tick over. This difficult period came to a sudden end in 1887, with new orders, the implementation of new safety requirements, and the run-up to the final conversion from broad to standard gauge in 1892. As the national recession drew to a close in the mid-1890s the GWR was poised to set new standards of comfort and sophistication, with improved locomotive and carriage design, and an assured future for Swindon at the head of railway technology.

Clearly, in charting the progress of the railway works to the dawn of the new century, when it employed over 11,500 (most of them male breadwinners), we have accounted for much of Swindon's spectacular rise in population. A few years later, in 1908, it was estimated that nearly 80% of Swindon's male workforce were employed by the GWR. So many men inside the works left a pool of employable wives and daughters outside, and this attracted clothing factories to Swindon. The largest, Compton's in Sheppard Street, had 1,000 employees in the 1890s, and very appropriately its work included the manufacture of GWR uniforms. Even so, relatively few Swindon women (7.2% in 1908) were in paid employment.

What about the men who did not work 'inside' (as employment in the railway works was always referred to), or elsewhere on the railway system? Some at Old Town were quarrymen, or were connected with the agriculture of the surrounding area. Many more worked in the various retail and service industries which the growing town required. A particular need, of course, was for houses to accommodate the multitude of newcomers, and an army of building workers moved in. They were the true creators of Victorian Swindon, and much of their legacy remains to the present day.

Sir John Betjeman was commissioned to write a study of architecture in Swindon to commemorate the combined borough's half-century in 1950. From the beautifully polished essay which resulted we may gather that he found the town interesting, but unattractive. He drew a clear distinction between architecture, of which he discovered few examples and little to admire, and building, of which he found a great deal, and much to criticize. But in his 1950 work

Looking south down Rodbourne Road the building to the left, now one side of the Factory Outlet, is part of the 1870s locomotive works. To the right is the pattern store of 1897, surmounted by massive water tanks.

Late Victorian houses marching up Eastcott Hill towards Old Town from New Swindon below

he could not be too rude about his paymasters' town. In another essay published in 1952 he was more blunt: 'For there is no doubt that Swindon *is* superficially ugly. That pretty model village of the eighteen-forties has developed a red brick rash which stretches up the hill to Old Swindon and strangles it.'

The 'red brick rash' is entirely the result of piecemeal and usually small-scale development by builders and speculators, who responded to the housing demands of the new population, and who, in the absence of any local government planning policy, were constrained only by market forces and the availability of land. A good example of this process at work is described in the autobiography of an influential education-alist, F H Spencer, who was born in 1870 in a house (no longer standing) adjoining what is now Regent Circus. Spencer recalls a character whom he called 'Old Charlie', a tallish, thin Yorkshireman, who had made money as a skilled mechanic at the works, and who had invested it during the 1850s in buying Upper Eastcott farmhouse and six small stone cottages that went with it. On to these he built a terrace of six brick houses and a small shop, which he let out to tenants. Spencer's parents lived in one of these houses for about thirty years, and he remembered as a teenager helping Old Charlie to work out the charges necessary to make a minimum of 7.5% on a gross outlay in cottage property.

Portrait of F H Spencer, from his autobiography published in 1938

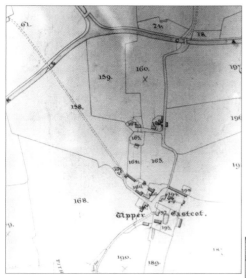

The Swindon tithe map of about 1840 (left) contrasts with the 1886 Ordnance Survey map (below) to show how the area around Eastcott Farm (now Regent Circus and Theatre Square) was developed during four decades. The field boundary between plots 158 and 168 became a major fault line when Commercial Road was developed a few years later (see map on page 65).

Charlie the Yorkshireman, who was 'no worse than the others' according to Spencer, called his terrace 'York Place'. Other speculators attained a kind of immortality for themselves and their families by enshrining them in street names. John Henry Harding Sheppard was a brewer in Old Town who owned land near the railway station and at Kingshill. Four streets in the Queens Town area between the railway village and the station divided up his name between them during the 1870s, and following his retirement to Kent we find a field at Kingshill being built up as Ashford, Folkestone, Hythe, Kent and Maidstone Roads. George Whitehead, as well as property speculator and builder, had careers as a shopkeeper, musician and publican. His wife Beatrice, his daughter Florence, and the composer after whom his shop was named, Handel, all have adjoining streets to themselves in Gorse Hill, but his own street, Whitehead Street, lies on the other side of the tracks, at least a ten-minute walk away – which, it has to be said, is a novel way of hinting at domestic disharmony.

Examples such as these could be multiplied from all over Victorian and Edwardian Swindon. For instance, the partners of an Old Town firm of solicitors, Messrs Butterworth, Rose, and Morrison, each have a street for their surnames, and George Montagu Butterworth and Sydney Bruce Morrison have both immortalized their middle names as well. More curiously, Edmund Jones built Maxwell Street, and James Maxwell built Edmund Street. Many other road names took their cue from the patriotic fervour of the later nineteenth century, or from national or GWR dignitaries. A few stem from allegiance to

John H H Sheppard's brewery in Old Town

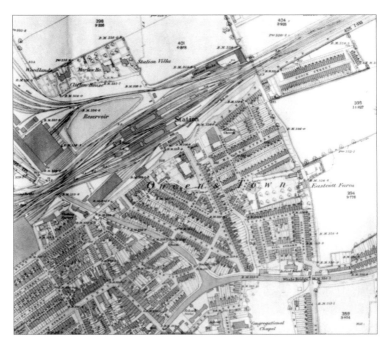

Piecemeal building development during the 1870s at Queen's Town, south and east of the railway station, as mapped by the Ordnance Survey in 1886. Houses were erected by private speculators and by building societies.

the builder's native place. Maxwell's firm came from Manchester (hence Manchester Road), Linslade Street was named by a native of the Bedfordshire town, Cheltenham and Gloucester Streets derive from the building society responsible, and there were two small neighbourhoods with Oxford overtones – Carfax, Merton, Oriel and Turl Streets; and Cobden, Harcourt and Iffley Roads – which were both the work of the Oxford Building Society and its successors.

'The people who planned these streets,' mused J B Priestley in disdain, as he explored Swindon on a dreary evening fifty years later, 'must have been thinking and dreaming hard about the next world, not this one: it is the only charitable conclusion.' But the reality was that they did very little planning at all, the majority of them lived elsewhere, and, like Old Charlie, they were thinking and dreaming mainly about their 7.5% return. They bid for individual plots of land or whole fields as they came on to the market, and either developed them immediately, if the works were booming and houses were in demand, or let them lie fallow for a few years, if economic conditions were less good. From sale catalogues, maps, directories and building byelaw records it is possible to trace their activities in great detail, but for present purposes a summary will suffice.

During the 1840s the railway village was the main area of growth, but speculative housing was already beginning to appear in the area of Westcott Place, following the line of a much older track known as the 'Fleet' or 'Fleetway'. And because railway works construction stimulated a temporary burst of activity at the canal wharf, a beerhouse and terrace of houses was built nearby. The beerhouse took its name, 'The Whale,' from the shape of the canal bridge next to it, and the houses, 'Cetus Buildings', took their rather pretentious name from the beerhouse (*cetus* is Latin for a whale). A second place of refreshment, the Golden Lion Inn, was in business by 1843, and this became a pivotal landmark in the development of the town's street plan. It stood beside the canal next to a swing-bridge, the Golden Lion Bridge, and from this a track led south-east across the field to Upper Eastcott Farm, and thence up Eastcott Hill to Old Swindon.

Golden Lion Bridge depicted on a mural painting adorning the side of a house near the site of Whale Bridge (now adjacent to Fleming Way)

Small workers' cottages of the 1850s along Regent Street survive and have been adapted for retail use, though now crowded out by much larger stores and offices

This bridge and track fixed the line of what was to become the next focus of private housing. During the 1850s terraces of small houses sprang up beside the track, which was then known along its whole length as Bridge Street. It was only later, during the 1860s and 1870s, that many of these houses were converted into shops, and then for the stretch of road south of Golden Lion Bridge a more stylish (even pretentious) name, Regent Street, was coined to reflect its new commercial status. The principal crossroad of the modern pedestrianized shopping centre now marks the site of the Golden Lion, but a few of the 1850s workers' houses still peep from behind and above shopfronts towards the southern end of Regent Street.

The Welsh Baptist chapel off Cambria Place, built to serve an influx of ironworkers during the 1860s from South Wales

Until the mid-1860s most of New Swindon, Regent Street apart, lay to the north of the Wilts and Berks Canal. Gooch's decision to build a rolling mill for iron rails at the works in 1861 attracted workers from the ironworks of South Wales. Initially they were housed with their families in the Barracks, but by 1864 a 'Welsh Colony' had been built for them between the railway village and Westcott Place. This was called Cambria Place, and had its own Welsh-speaking Baptist chapel. Further east, between the railway village and the angle formed by the junction of the North Wilts Canal with the Wilts and Berks, Mr Sheppard's field was built-up with the four roads of his name, John, Henry, Harding and Sheppard Streets.

It was a busy time for the railway works, as we have seen, with the new carriage works opening in 1868 and a full order book for locomotives continuing through much of the 1870s. These prosperous years, from about 1865 to 1877, found the property speculators and small-time builders busy too. Now a tide of red brick began to creep up the hill towards Old Swindon. Havelock Street and its neighbours now beneath the Brunel Plaza were followed by the advance guard of terraces around what became Regent Circus and the present Swindon College. Infilling occurred in the area between the railway village and the canal, now occupied by Farnsby Street and the Murray John tower. And forays were made eastward across the North Wilts Canal towards the station. But large areas of farmland around Swindon were out of bounds to developers until 1885, because of a legal dispute over the inheritance of what remained of one of Swindon's former manors, the Vilett estate. This restriction led, not only to overcrowding on cramped sites which were available, but also to sporadic housebuilding in far-flung places, such as on the slopes of Kingshill, and north of the railway at Even Swindon and Gorse Hill.

At the works the wheels of progress ground to a halt in about 1877, as we have seen, and the influx of new population was stemmed. The housebuilding market did not revive until after 1885, by when the restriction on Vilett lands had been lifted. This enforced lull, whatever its economic consequences at the time, offered a pause for reflection. New Swindon, from being a chaotic jumble of uncontrolled accretions for the accommodation of railway workers, was developing into an important town, with its own commercial and retail areas, a form of local government (New Swindon Board of Health), and a variety of social and welfare activities provided by, or connected with, the main employer.

One consequence of this was that, when building recommenced after 1885, schemes were on a larger and grander scale. Three developments set out to alter the balance of Swindon. The first lay to the west of Regent Street and was centred on a new alignment, Commercial Road. The aim of the builders was to capture from Regent Street its trading supremacy. A market was built at its western end, where it met the canal, and at the eastern end Regent Circus was laid out by 1889, around a blatantly municipal building, the town hall of 1891. The second scheme involved forging a proper link with the old town by creating a thoroughfare up the hill. Victoria Road, as it was christened, was made up in 1888, and by 1900

This remarkable map (in WSRO) shows the effect of the release of the Vilett estate for housing and retail development, which was aligned on the new Commercial Road. Everything south of the 'fault line' (an old property boundary seen on the tithe map (see page 61) has been hand-drawn on to the printed Ordnance Survey map. The effect of this disjunction can still be seen today in Havelock Street (bottom picture, looking south) and its neighbours. The datestone (below) is fixed to a shop in Commercial Road.

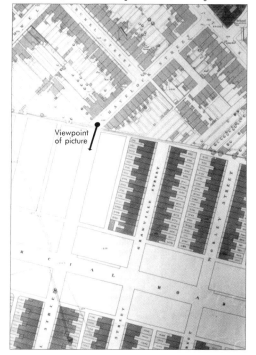

Viewpoint of picture

houses and side streets had been built along much of its length. The third large-scale development, which took place during the years around 1900, filled with houses the area between the station and the canal, aligned on Manchester Road and Broad Street.

Alongside these giant modifications to the Swindon landscape the small opportunist builder continued his work of infilling odd plots and poking out into the suburbs. Furthermore – and this is often overlooked – Old Swindon too was growing, especially on its northern and western edges. Here, according to Betjeman, we shall encounter the Victorian middle classes: 'Outcast from the most exclusive sets of the Old Town, houses will be coming tripping down Eastcott Hill and Prospect Hill and the Bath Road on their way to New Swindon. Rising on the railway boom, the more fortunate of the mechanics will climb the hill to greet them.'

Prospect Place, Old Town. Old Swindon spread down the hill in the nineteenth century, just as New Swindon spread up the hill

In a poem written several years before his Swindon essay Betjeman described such houses as, 'brick-built breeding boxes of new souls'. To his subtle eye the little differences of detail and architectural gradations of Swindon houses from street to street and area to area reflect all the nuances of English social class. Bricks and mortar remain as mute evidence of the pretensions of their builders, and the aspirations of first and subsequent occupants. Observant pedestrians on their way down Victoria Road will notice such things; in particular they may spot the plaque recording the fact that Richard Jefferies lived for a year in one of the houses.

House in Victoria Road where Richard Jefferies lived. The plaque is between the first floor windows.

Jefferies was a man of the countryside, not the town, and to categorize him on the basis of his house as an aspiring middle-class Victorian seems somehow inadequate. Born at Coate in 1848 he was one of the last of thousands of Swindonians to be baptized at the old

Richard Jefferies (1848-1887), prose-poet of the English countryside *par excellence*; and the view across Coate Water, beside which he was born, and the setting for many episodes and descriptions in his writings

parish church of Holy Rood (in January 1849) before its replacement by Christ Church in 1851. After a spell as a local journalist he supported himself and his family by writing novels and essays, until his premature death from tuberculosis in 1887. Interest in his work, never entirely extinguished, has revived from time to time, during the 1940s and 1970s, and now, with renewed interest in ecology and nature conservation, some of his books on country life and natural history are holding their place as classics of the genre. Recent opposition to building development at Coate, his old stamping ground, has thrust him back into the local limelight as well. His output included work on local history, and we may claim him as Swindon's first historian, although this was not his forte. But, like Betjeman, he was interested in the sociology of the town, and his observations on Swindon in 1867 are astute.

Jefferies drew a distinction between 'the lower class of mechanics, especially the factory labourers', on the one hand, who were local men from the surrounding villages attracted to the works by higher wages; and the class of 'educated mechanics', on the other – well travelled, intelligent, eager to debate, read and learn. This latter group, 'in reality the protoplasm, or living matter, out of which modern society is evolved', were incomers to New Swindon, and their presence leavened the social life and character of the town. They ate meat and lived well, relatively speaking, but were not guilty of excesses; because they expected a regular income they tended to spend their money rather than save. This trait, in the eyes of Jefferies the farmer's son, was a grave character defect, but it resulted from a generous, liberal disposition, always ready to buy a friend a drink, take the family for a jaunt, or treat a daughter to a new dress. 'The mechanic does not set a value upon money in itself.'

This assessment accords precisely with F.H. Spencer's memory of his father, a precision engineer at the works who was descended from a Lancashire family of small landowners. A quiet, thoughtful man, 'with an unexhibited pride at the root of his nature', he had a passion for books, and for visiting abbeys and cathedrals to study their architecture. There was a second-hand piano in the house, and one of the children had a violin. But – and here Jefferies' stricture rings true – 'We were slightly in debt. The rent was always a few weeks in arrear, and there was an ancient butcher's bill incurred during the long stay of convalescent relatives in a distant past, which we gradually liquidated by occasional half-crowns.'

Spencer contrasts this household of culture, intellect and decency with the miserable condition of the rented house itself. This too has an echo in the observations of Jefferies. In one of his novels, *Greene Ferne Farm* published in 1880, we follow a curate about his visits in 'Kingsbury', alias New Swindon. 'At the end of a new street hastily "run up cheap" and "scamped", they found a large black pool, once a pond in the meadow, now a slough of all imaginable filth, at whose precipitous edge the roadway stopped abruptly.' Upstairs in one of these 'scamped' six-roomed houses, with doors that warped and would not shut, they visited a young man recuperating from an accident at the works, lying on his bed in a sickly, fetid room in the middle of a summer day. He was one of the 'lower class of mechanics' arrived from a nearby village, and had been an under-shepherd. Now from his squalid surroundings he was staring out at lambs in a nearby field through a window that could not be made to open.

We suggested earlier that, during the doldrums of the late 1870s when this description was written, New Swindon had a respite, and took stock of its progress before beginning to organize itself as a proper town. In fact some urban trappings had already been in place for a number of years. Shops, schools, pubs and chapels sprang up throughout the town in the wake of new housing, and supplemented the medical, recreational and cultural facilities associated with the GWR. And both old and new towns had had their separate boards of health since 1864. The New Swindon Local Board organized gas street lamps, and began a rudimentary sewerage system. Although this was gradually improved and refined it continued for many years to demonstrate its shortcomings in various offensive ways, such as the slough of filth depicted by Jefferies. Later came a piped water supply from waterworks at Wroughton, and various public health and protection measures followed.

During the early years the two town boards refused to co-operate with each other, but gradually commonsense prevailed, and matters of joint concern, such as firefighting, and the provision of a cemetery and an isolation hospital, were tackled together. During the building boom of the 1890s the conclusion became inevitable that Old and New Swindon should be governed together, and this was probably anticipated in the positioning of the New Swindon Local Board's offices at Regent

The offices of New Swindon Local Board was built in 1891, and became the town hall and centre of administration of the Borough of Swindon in 1900, when the two towns were amalgamated. The coat of arms of the incorporated borough (below) included a railway locomotive.

Circus in 1891 – the town hall, as it became, was sited roughly halfway between the original nuclei of the two towns. During the 1890s amalgamation and incorporation as a borough became a burning local issue, and in 1897 the Privy Council was petitioned for Swindon to obtain its charter. On 9th November 1900, a little over sixty years after Gooch and Brunel had finished their picnic, the Borough of Swindon became a reality.

6 EVENING STAR AND SUNRISE

GASLIGHT IN THE LIVING ROOM, harmonium in the front parlour, and bowler hat hanging in the hall – the home life of the successful railway worker in about 1900 was beautifully re-created at 34 Faringdon Road, the foreman's cottage which in 1980 was turned into the railway village museum (but now, unfortunately, closed). James Hall, a second-generation Swindon railwayman, lived there in modest comfort with his wife and family, in the house which his parents had moved into when it was new and he was a child, forty years before in about 1860.

Within a short stroll from his back door was (or in 1900 would shortly be) a bewildering range of services and facilities provided by local government, 'the company', private enterprise and self-help. There were shops and pubs, a covered market and the mechanics' institute (with its enterprising range of social and cultural activities), churches and chapels, a hospital and swimming baths, and schools for the children. A theatre (the Queen's, later the Empire) had been built in 1898, some twenty working-men's clubs had opened between 1880 and 1900, professional football at the County Ground had begun in 1895, and there had been a local evening paper since 1882. A railway line connecting

The entrance to the GWR Medical Fund swimming baths and dispensary in Faringdon Road. Built in 1891 it offered a range of health-related facilities.

The Mechanics' Institute was the heart of the railway village, sketched here in 1914

Old and New Swindon (part of the Midland and South Western Junction Railway from Cheltenham to Andover) was built in 1881-3. A few years' later, in 1903, the new borough council would take over the running of its schools, and also begin university extension lectures. During the same year an electricity works was built, and it generated power not only for electric street lighting, but also for a tramway system which started running services in 1904.

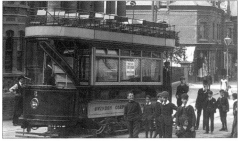

A Swindon tramcar at the top of Regent Street in about 1905

Everything – all these trappings of successful urban growth – was a product of the previous sixty years, and had grown up with the railway works, on which it all still ultimately depended for its existence. But during the twentieth century new themes emerged – the decline and fall of the works; the industries which came to replace them; and the overspill world of the suburbs.

The fate of the works may be gauged in statistics. The workforce had reached 14,000 by 1905, and peaked in 1925 at 14,369. In 1930 it was 11,500, and in 1939 10,500. After 1945 it remained fairly constant at about 10,000 until 1960, but had fallen to 8,000 in 1962, and 5,100 in 1967. A low point of 2,200 was reached in 1973, but thereafter it rose to 3,800 by 1980, before dropping to just over 1,000 before closure in 1986. It has been suggested that at the start of the century the GWR division based at Swindon, which was responsible for locomotives, carriages and wagons, as well as their drivers and firemen (a grand total of about 17,000 employees), was probably the largest undertaking in British, and perhaps European, industry at the time. With the opening of a new carriage store in 1938 the works reached their maximum geographical extent, more than 326 acres, including 79 acres roofed over.

Another way of looking at things is to consider the output of the works, and the legendary names of railway history responsible for designing and producing the famous locomotives built at Swindon. In 1901 G J Churchward, deputy and superintendent-elect, produced on a single sheet of paper the

City of Truro, built at Swindon in 1903. It achieved 100 mph the following year

diagrams for six new types of locomotive, which employed a revolutionary boiler design. During his time in office (he retired as superintendent in 1921) five of these types went into production; they became the GWR's workhorses, and earned enviable reputations for speed and reliability. Developments in carriage and wagon design also went on apace, and the ingenious designers and engineers in the works continued to show that they could turn their hand to any problem – in 1891 they had patented a cake-cutting machine for the annual children's fête, and in 1914 they built a pagoda-like advertising kiosk for use at agricultural shows, which still survives as a refreshment stall in the Town Gardens. Churchward played an influential part too in the life of the town. He was the borough's mayor in the year of incorporation, and its first honorary freeman. After his retirement he continued to live in a house near the railway works until his death (run down by an express train while examining a loose rail) in 1933.

Part of a plan of the railway works in 1935, shortly before it reached its greatest extent

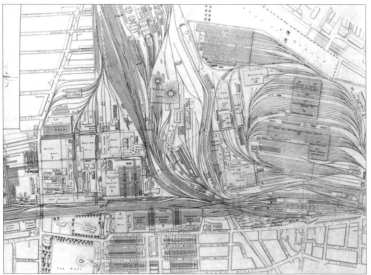

C B Collett, Churchward's successor, was responsible for developing many of the most famous classes of GWR locomotive, including

The refreshment pagoda in Town Gardens was made in the railway workshops as a GWR advertising kiosk

'Castles', 'Kings', 'Granges', 'Manors' and 'Halls'. His term of office (1922-41) also included the first experiments with diesel traction. On 1 January 1948 The GWR ceased to exist, and the nationalized British Railways took over the works, but steam locomotive production continued through the 1950s alongside new diesel-hydraulic units. The last steam locomotive to be built for British Railways emerged from the works on 18 March 1960, and was named 'Evening Star'. Diesel-hydraulic traction was phased out during the 1960s in favour of diesel-electric; this jeopardized Swindon's future, and by 1970 it seemed likely that British Rail Engineering Ltd (as it had become) would close the works. The gloom was premature, and it was not until 1985, while Swindon was preparing to celebrate the 150th anniversary of the founding of the GWR, that closure was announced, with effect from 26 March 1986. Commemoration gave way to anger, and the celebrations were abandoned.

'I had never been to Swindon before, and all I knew about it was that the Great Western Railway had its chief works there and that it made the best railway engines in the world.' So wrote J B Priestley when he visited the town in 1933. It was quite true, of course, and Swindon was proud of it. But civic pride had, by the 1930s, become tempered with a kind of malaise, which manifested itself in several ways. Priestley found the shops shoddy, the houses monotonous and the food in the eating-house dubious. As he trudged the damp, dark, autumnal town after dinner, and found it murky, with an unfriendly, shuttered look, he mused on 'these smaller industrial towns, where you can work but cannot really play'. Betjeman detected the same malaise in the new building of the inter-war years, which made Swindon, he said, look like any industrial suburb anywhere. And Kenneth Hudson, writing much later, during the 1960s, made himself very unpopular locally by suggesting that to the outside world, 'the name

Swindon almost automatically conveyed the idea of somewhere out-of-date, small, mean and stick-in-the-mud,' and that this was, 'an important, if sad, part of the legacy of the railway town; it was a burden the town appeared to have to carry'. Hudson suggested a change of name to dispel the image, and provoked a storm of protest – yet Thamesdown Borough Council was less than a decade away.

An obvious explanation for the malaise is that it began when the works and the town stopped expanding at the phenomenal rate of the first sixty years. And it is precisely then, during the Edwardian years, that we first detect it, in a locally famous book, *Life in a Railway Factory*, by a locally famous author, Alfred Williams. Williams was a product of the mechanics' institute ethos of self-improvement for the working man by education. Poet, folksong collector, lover of the countryside, and student of ancient languages, he worked as a steam-hammerman at the works from 1893 until poor health ended his arduous career in 1914. He wrote his description of the works in 1911, but it was not published until 1915. It offers a detailed picture of the working environment, including all the dangers and hardships, the victimization and practical jokes. It is a powerful book by an embittered employee who, it must be admitted, is blatantly unsympathetic to the GWR. Much of the abuse and horseplay which he describes was harmless – apprentices, for instance, were misled by their older workmates into believing that they all had to be branded on one buttock with a large G, and on the other with a W (the company initials), using a hot iron stamp. But Williams also described a deteriorating relationship between shopfloor and management, as new machinery was introduced, bureaucracy increased, and the quest for greater efficiency imposed ever stiffer burdens on the workforce.

Alfred Williams, the hammerman poet

This increased tension in labour relations (by no means unique to Swindon at this time) which the disaffected Alfred Williams chronicled in his book is reflected also in the growth of union membership. A Swindon Trades Council was formed in 1891 to represent the various unions in the town, and it claimed that its membership of 1,000 in 1892 and 2,000 in 1903 had risen by 1917 to 10,000. The Trades Council put up candidates to local councils, including one man, Reuben George, who went on to become mayor and alderman of Swindon, and a county councillor, dying in 1936. A larger-than-life character, and champion of the Workers' Educational Association, he became one of Swindon's folk-heroes, along with the philanthropic rag-and-bone man, James 'Raggy' Powell, and David Murray John, town clerk from 1937 to 1974. In complete contrast to the shabby image Swindon may have had among outsiders, their whole-hearted commitment to the town has given it a tangible civic pride and dignity which became a very notable feature of its twentieth-century history.

As expansion and prosperity at the works became less dependable during and after the First World War, the borough and trades councils realized that Swindon had to diversify, and attract new industries into the town. Early arrivals – the clothing workshops already described, as well as Wills' tobacco factory in 1915, and Garrard Engineering in 1919 – were all chiefly employers of women, so did not provide a direct substitute for the railway works. In fact as numbers at the works began to decline during the 1930s many engineering workers found employment at Morris Motors in Cowley, Oxford, and commuted there from Swindon by train on a daily basis. Vickers Armstrong, who arrived at South Marston in 1937/8, was followed by other large engineering and electrical concerns during the Second World War, such as Plessey and R A Lister. Such were the employment opportunities in the town during the war, in fact, that immigration had to be limited, and Swindon was designated a closed area which civilians could not enter without permission.

Swindon council activists (left to right): James 'Raggy' Powell, Reuben George and G J Churchward

Three new elements emerged after the war to complicate the process of expansion and diversification. First was the development of forward planning at local and national level. This meant that the opportunist piecemeal growth of the town in response to the needs of employers was a thing of the past. From now on its course would be master-minded. Second was the problem that Swindon, within its existing boundaries, was full up, and any further expansion would encroach on the neighbouring local authority – Highworth Rural District Council – and affect Wiltshire County Council. There was a long-standing antipathy between Swindon and the rest of Wiltshire, which grew worse after 1974, when many local government services were transferred to the county. 'Trowbridge' (Wiltshire's county town) became a dirty word in Swindon, and periodical outbreaks of hostility continued until 1997, when the Swindon area achieved the status of a unitary authority, and so became largely independent of the county. Third was government policy, which at first favoured the creation of new towns, but after 1951 preferred the controlled growth of

existing centres as 'overspill' towns. Swindon
was designated a London overspill town on 25
June 1952, and this had a profound effect on its
subsequent development.

The industrial and employment
consequences, which we should look at first, were
that numerous engineering, electrical, scientific
and distributive companies opened plants in and
around Swindon during the 1950s and 1960s.
They included one, Pressed Steel, which by 1965
had a larger workforce at its Stratton premises
than the railway works. By 1970, encouraged in
particular by the borough council's vigorous
promotion of itself to potential employers, there
were over 35,000 manufacturing jobs in Swindon.
Many were located in units on council-initiated
trading and industrial estates. Expansion
continued during the 1970s, although the main
growth now was in service and white-collar
industries. A temporary check during the early
1980s was followed by a dramatic upturn in
Swindon's fortunes, especially in what were then
being called the 'sunrise' industries, of
computers, electronics and information
technology. The startling architecture of
Swindon's 1980s new image greets the visitor
along the western access road from the
motorway – the motorway (opened in 1971)
which was one of its chief progenitors.

The headquarters of
W H Smith at
Greenbridge

Hand in hand with the town's policy of
diversified employment has been the
suburbanization of Swindon, and this is the
final theme in our summary of twentieth-
century history. In chapter five we left Swindon
in around 1900 at the point where the two
towns had coalesced, and redbrick had sprawled
haphazardly around them in most directions.
But Swindon's Victorian housing development
was not really suburban, rather it was a series of

small accretions and piecemeal infillings, often on rather cramped sites. This process continued until 1914, with new housing concentrated on the Okus, Kingshill and quarry areas west of Old Town, the Broad Street district near the station, and north of the tracks at Gorse Hill and Even Swindon. After the First World War Swindon began to march out into the countryside.

During the 1920s and 1930s, here as everywhere, there were two types of housing, council and private. In general terms council houses were sturdier, built to better specifications, and more imaginatively positioned on estates. The overriding concern for private housebuilders and occupiers, rooted in class snobbery, was that their houses should not look like council houses; in other respects economies were made, and this included so-called ribbon development along existing main roads, which saved expense on building the infrastructure of estate roads and services. Swindon expanded northwards, with a council estate at Pinehurst, and private housing at Rodbourne. The Pinehurst estate was laid out on a circular plan by one of the pioneers of the garden city movement, Sir Raymond Unwin (although he was not responsible for the design of the houses), and its tree-named streets were

A former distribution depot for Renault, employing a revolutionary form of roof construction. It was erected at West Swindon in 1983 but is now disused

Pinehurst Circle

Inter-war ribbon development along Marlborough Road, Lawn

gradually built up between the wars. In addition to the Rodbourne estate private housing ribboned along the main roads radiating from Old Town. In 1928 much of the ancient parish of Rodbourne Cheney was absorbed within the borough boundary, and part of Stratton St Margaret was taken as well.

Swindon's population in 1901, we recall, was 45,000, and this had been a ninefold increase during the previous fifty years. By 1951 it had reached 69,000 – a substantial increase, but on nothing like the scale of the nineteenth century. Decade by decade between 1901 and 1951 the average growth was less than 10%, a comfortable rate of expansion which these suburban adventures could readily accommodate. But after 1945, and especially after the London overspill decision in 1952, the rate of growth increased again, with a consequent need for carefully planned suburban expansion. Between 1951 and 1961 another 23,000 people came to live in Swindon, nearly as many in ten years as in the previous fifty. But they were only the tip of an anticipated iceberg. Plans produced during the 1960s envisaged growth to 180,000, 200,000, 230,000, even 400,000 by the end of the century. The 200,000 estimate, suggested in 1968, became the accepted target.

Cavendish Square, Park South

Until the 1952 decision, Swindon's post-war housing effort had been concentrated, as before, to the north of the town. To these years principally belong the suburbs of Moredon and Penhill. But from 1952 a massive expansion to the east began. Walcot East and Walcot West came first, separated not only by a new dual-carriageway road, Queen's Drive of 1953, but also by the English class system, which was still endeavouring to distinguish between council and private houses. Next came private housing at Lawn, and council housing at Park North and South. And with them, in the early 1960s, Swindon's boundaries were full up again, and further expansion had to encroach on its neighbours. Meanwhile those neighbours were themselves growing rapidly. The two rural districts bordering Swindon (Cricklade and Wootton Bassett, and Highworth) grew by a total of nearly 20,000 population between 1951 and 1966, and one parish, Stratton St Margaret, returned a population of 19,400 at the 1971 census, which was larger than most Wiltshire towns.

The Link Centre, West Swindon

The key planning document of the 1960s, the so-called 'Silver Book', spawned further suburban housing and industrial expansion. Initially this was concentrated to the east, at Liden, Nythe, Covingham, Dorcan and Eldene, where gradual infilling took place up to the line of the Stratton St Margaret by-pass (our old friend the Roman road). But during the 1980s an entirely new area was opened up west of Swindon, and this was developed as a self-contained community, with its own facilities.

Meanwhile radical changes were taking place in the town centre, as Victorian cottages were demolished to make way for pedestrianized shopping precincts. Here the inspiration was an influential report by the distinguished town planner, Sir Colin Buchanan, published in 1963,

The entance to the Brunel Plaza from Canal Walk

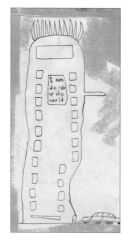

Young artist's portrayal of the Murray John Tower (I think), spotted on a community arts mural in Fleming Way, 2005

which recommended segregating traffic and pedestrians by removing cars from town centre shopping streets. Canal Walk was created as a pedestrian shopping street on the line of the Wilts & Berks Canal. To its south the Brunel Centre or Plaza, a covered shopping mall, was opened in 1972 and included a supermarket and multiple stores. Traffic was diverted away from the central streets by the creation of Fleming Way, which also gave access to multi-storey car parks. Regent Street and Bridge Street became traffic-free. Rising from amidst this retail forest a 22-storey tower block of offices and flats was erected, and named (most appropriately) after David Murray John, Swindon's visionary town clerk who had initiated most of the borough's post-war achievements. It has become Swindon's icon.

The Magic Roundabout, nicknamed after a children's television series of the 1960s and 1970s, has become famous or infamous far beyond Swindon. It is part of the traffic management scheme which takes vehicles along Fleming Way and around the predestrianized shopping area. The County Ground football stadium floodlights can be seen in the background.

7 NO MEAN CITY?

As PART of her golden jubilee commemorations in 2002 the Queen graciously agreed not to grant Swindon the status of a city. She had reached the same decision two years earlier when celebrating the millennium. It was another sad day for Swindon's not-to-be citizens, mitigated only by the news that their arch-rival Reading had been similarly rejected. It was long odds – only one out of the twenty-six applications from English towns could be successful – and city status is, after all, purely honorific. But success would have set a kind of royal seal of approval on how much Swindon had achieved in recent decades, and failure was, well, failure – especially when set against Her Majesty's stated criteria, which included historical features, regional and national significance and a forward-looking attitude. So, having spent six chapters of our book challenging the notion that Swindon has no worthwhile history, our postscript should bring the town's saga into the new century by looking at significance and attitude. What about those engines of growth – the new employers, the retailers and the unitary council – those burgeoning suburbs, and those changes, both subtle and radical, at the heart? What do they tell us about Swindon now, and for the future?

Swindon at work, in the 1980s, was a mix of manufacturing, service and so-called 'sunrise' industries. Two decades on there is still this mix, though new ingredients have been added and the quantities have changed. In parallel with national trends manufacturing industries have declined, but here Honda's arrival at South Marston in 1989, and the Japanese company's major investment in new plant in 2001, seem to have assured for Swindon a long-term career as a car-making centre of international significance. Financial institutions, notably Allied Dunbar and Nationwide, came here in the 1970s and have subsequently dug in, with new headquarters and expanding workforces. Butter,

National Trust headquarters building opened on the railway works site in 2005

books, pills, mobile phones, car and computer bits, oil, railway services, compact discs, electricity, and a host of other requirements – as like as not the producing or supplying company has its head office in Swindon. And alongside these captains of commerce a new species has arrived, the quango. Following on from the government research councils, who migrated here during the 1970s, the National Monuments Record (now part of English Heritage) came in 1994, and has been joined in 2005, as eco-friendly next-door neighbour on the railway works site, by the headquarters of the National Trust.

Bravo Swindon! On the scale of social kudos hosting the National Trust probably ranks higher than achieving city status. But, as in 1840, so in 2000, new employers mean new patterns of employment. Three points should be made which affect Swindon's significance and attitude. First, a considerable though unquantified proportion of the new workforce does not live in or feel any allegiance to Swindon, but commutes – in many cases from considerable distances. Second, the balance of male and female employment has undoubtedly

The National Monuments Record Centre of English Heritage, housed in the GWR general offices building since its refurbishment in 1992-4

Futuristic office building overlooking the lake at Roughmoor, West Swindon. Ranks of computers are visible inside, but the building is currently (2005) unused.

shifted, offering a welcome and healthy equality, but also a challenge to traditional attitudes. And third, many of the new employers are multi-national companies, offering Swindon its chance to shine on the global stage, but also leaving it susceptible to globally distant boardroom politics.

Earning it is one thing, spending it is another. The town centre's pedestrian streets and Brunel Plaza, so radical in the 1970s, were looking tired by the 1990s, and ready for the facelift they received in 1995-7. A new covered market was created and, near the site of its predecessor, a large department store was built by a high-class chain. Shortly afterwards, in 1998, Swindon's home-grown department store, McIlroys, which had been trading in Regent Street since the Victorian period, closed its doors and was swiftly demolished. Plans under way in 2005 envisage,

Refurbishment of the pedestrianized shopping centre during the 1990s took on a parasol theme. The structures (left) adorn The Parade, and afford useful protection from the elements, as does the roof of the covered market (below).

not so much cosmetic surgery for the town centre, more a heart and lung transplant, as new vital organs replace the old, with fanciful and contemporary names, Hub, Arena, Campus, Promenade, Exchange.

Townscape renewal at the historic centre is one of several ways in which Swindon mirrors urban trends elsewhere. Another is the emergence of retail parks. In Swindon a former industrial estate at Greenbridge was converted for retailing by the council during the 1990s, and a peripheral 'out-of-town' park opened beside a major road junction at Gablecross near South Marston. The district centres of West and North Swindon have evolved in similar fashion, with superstores and multiples taking root alongside smaller businesses and community facilities. Most imaginative has been the conversion of much of the 1870s locomotive works into the 'McArthurGlen Great Western Designer Outlet', a complex of around 100 shops offering discounted goods, within an ambience

Food mall in the Great Western Designer outlet, formerly part of the 1870s locomotive works (as may be inferred from its principal occupant)

of preserved railway rolling stock and heavy engineering. Trumpeted in 1997 when it opened as the country's largest retail regeneration project, this shoppers' paradise has created for itself a catchment area far wider than Swindon and its immediate neighbours.

If employment and retailing have been two engines of Swindon's growth, the third has been autonomy. April 1997 saw the death of Thamesdown, a district within and subordinate to the county of Wiltshire, and the birth of Swindon Borough Council, a unitary authority with sole responsibility for almost all aspects of its local government. The future for Swindon became orange, as a new livery was emblazoned all over signs and public buildings. Orange, but not gold, as freedom, long wished and striven for, proved neither panacea nor utopia. The cost of restructuring, shortfalls in government-imposed spending levels, and critical reports of under-performance, all dented the slogan 'proud to be Swindon'. In response to its problems the New Swindon Company, an urban regeneration partnership, was formed in 2002 to revitalize the town centre, and the council itself issued a recovery plan and published a series of promises to improve its services between 2005 and 2010.

Hoarding on the site of the former post office premises off Fleming Way, proclaiming in 2005 the regeneration programme

Meanwhile Swindon has continued to expand. The vision of the 'Silver Book' of 1968 was that suburban development should take place to the east (the Eldene and Liden area and South Marston), to the west (Toothill, Westlea, Freshbrook and Shaw), and to the north (the so-called Haydon sector); and that within each should be built a series of 'urban villages', or neighbourhoods. Ruefully one may reflect on the nature of Swindon's encrypting and decoding that, when we spoke in chapter 2 of an 'urban village', we meant that the medieval hilltop settlement was trying to turn itself into a small town. Now we find the same oxymoronic phrase cropping up again, but this time to mean the opposite – a very large town trying to turn itself into an accumulation of villages.

Though endlessly modified as to timing, extent, responsibility and finance, and the subject of numerous subsequent reports, the actual geography of Swindon's suburbs has turned out much as the 1968 planners envisaged it. Eldene and Liden were built in the early 1970s, as we have seen, and work began at West Swindon, with the creation of Toothill between 1974 and 1979. A planning inquiry sanctioned development of the other West Swindon neighbourhoods in 1978, but because of recession and financial restraints, housebuilding proceeded much more slowly than had been envisaged, and took nearly twenty years to complete.

Orbital Retail Park, North Swindon, the Wal-Mart superstore building

Development of the Haydon sector, to the north and west of Swindon's older suburbs at Moredon and Penhill, was politically contentious during the 1980s, and a protracted and unsettled period ensued, of planning applications, building consortia, revised forecasts and planning inquiries, before construction began in 1995. An orbital road, Thamesdown Drive, was built to act as a conduit, linking the 'villages' to each other, to their North Swindon District Centre (the Orbital Retail Park), and to the outside world. Work in 2005 is still in progress, and the new communities, with their anodyne names – Abbey Meads, Priory Vale, Taw Hill, St Andrew's Ridge – are beginning to establish themselves. In conception they are quite different from those in West Swindon, so that anyone venturing into the furthermost reaches, between Thamesdown Drive and Tadpole Lane, will find a pastiche of every imaginable (and unimaginable) style of domestic architecture, from Cotswold cottage to Regency crescent.

New housing, in Georgian town centre style, at Priory Vale, North Swindon

With the Silver Book's vision almost realized, new planning battle lines have been drawn. The principal theatre of conflict since 1995 has been Swindon's so-called 'front garden' or 'gateway', extending from the eastern motorway junction across Badbury Wick to Coate Water – the very fields immortalized by Richard Jefferies.

Swindon's first crescent? New housing in North Swindon

Development has also been proposed in the Westleaze and Westlecott area south-west of Old Town (likewise confined by the motorway), and in the east, beyond Liden and Dorcan. But none of these schemes has yet turned into bricks and mortar.

As a conurbation of 200,000 people, home of iconic employers, and shopping magnet for a wide region, Swindon's significance is hardly in question. What about that other quality, far more difficult to define – attitude? We have already touched on some of the factors that shape a community's attitudes – autonomy, regeneration, expansion. And there are other straws in the wind.

When the columnist Miles Kington referred in jest to 'the Bishop of Swindon' was he perhaps subconsciously recalling a rude limerick I once heard about 'the Bishop of Crewe'? What he did not realize, and what other Swindon detractors would be surprised to learn, is that the Right Reverend Michael Doe was indeed appointed as the first Bishop of Swindon in 1994. He became a leading crusader for city-status, but there is no talk of a cathedral yet!

The Oakfield Campus of the University of Bath in Swindon

Another status symbol, however, is becoming a reality. Various attempts were begun in the 1990s to create a 'University of Swindon', including a scheme to link the former Royal Military College of Science at Shrivenham and Cranfield Institute of Technology, and to form a science park on the town's northern outskirts. This fell through in 1995, and what has emerged in fact is a Swindon presence of the University of Bath, based in existing college buildings at Oakfield, between Greenbridge and Park. Current plans to develop a university campus in more sequestered surroundings near Coate Water are contentious, not because Swindon rejects the notion of a university, but because of the sensitivity of the chosen site.

Long proud, and rightly so, of its public parks, the greening of Swindon leapt forward in 1990 with the establishment of the Great Western Community Forest. This embraces various ecological initiatives, including tree-planting, the creation of the Mouldon Hill country park west of Haydon . . . Cycle ways, park-and-ride schemes, the restoration of parts of the Wilts & Berks Canal, and the designation of a nature reserve at Haydon Meadow and a scheduled ancient monument on Groundwell Ridge, all suggest that Swindon, if not pioneering in, is at least conforming to the prevailing climate of environmental sensitivity.

STEAM, the Museum of the Great Western Railway, is housed in a former works building of 1865, which incorporates a wall from Brunel's original engine house

In its cultural life the programmes of the Arts Centre in Old Town and the Wyvern Theatre have been joined since 1994 by an annual Festival of Literature. The long-promised new central library is still a promise, but now the promise has a completion date – 2008. Another long hoped-for ambition has been realized, with the opening in 2000 of STEAM, a museum devoted to the town's railway heritage, offering stunning displays and artefacts contained within buildings of the former railway works.

If the Queen's decision in 2002 about city status was a disappointment, for many in Swindon it pales into insignificance compared with another decision, taken a dozen years earlier, in June 1990, by the Football Association. Swindon Town Football Club, a rallying call of local patriotism since it turned professional in 1894, had for the first time in its history just achieved promotion to what is now the premier division of the league. But tricky footwork off the pitch, on the balance sheet, was punished by demotion. Picking itself up by its bootstraps the club was promoted once more in 1993, but only remained in the premier league for one season.

It is now forty years since Kenneth Hudson researched his sociological study of Swindon 'at the 100,000 mark', and the population has doubled since then. *An Awkward Size for a Town*, published in 1967, described in great detail the living standards and aspirations of 1960s Swindonians. The dowdy image of the railway terraces had not then been shaken off, the shopping malls of the town centre were not complete, the Wyvern Theatre had not been built, the 'hi-tech' industries were decades away, the railway works were still a powerful force. Replying to a questionnaire about his ambitions a sixth-former replied in terms of the initials he wanted to see after his name – BSc, PhD, FRS, OBE, 'and having made this clear, said he doubted if Swindon was going to be big enough to hold him'. He will be coming up to his pension now. Has Swindon thrown off its awkwardness, and become big enough in significance and attitude (as well as geographically) to have held him? Has he achieved his ambitions yet? And has Swindon?

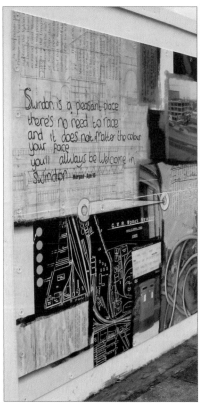

Children's community art attached to hoardings around a building site in Fleming Way, 2005

8 A JOURNEY OF DISCOVERY ~~~ OLD & NEW SWINDON

This journey begins at the Market Square in Old Town, and after exploring the hilltop settlement descends by Eastcott Hill to New Swindon. From Regent Street it follows the course of the canal to Cambria Place, the railway village and former works. It ends at Fleming Way, from where a regular bus service runs back up to Old Town. Pay and display car parking is available close to the start of the walk. An option to shorten the tour, by exploring Old Town only, is indicated in the text; readers wishing to confine their walk to New Swindon should begin at Regent Circus on page 95. Pedestrian crossings and road crossings with dropped kerbs are used wherever possible, and possible difficulties and alternatives for wheelchair users are described. A map showing all the twists and turns of this journey is printed on the last page of this book, inside the back cover (page 104).

Throughout this journey instructions about the route are given in bold type. The paragraph(s) of description which follow instructions usually relate to features visible at points along this part of the route, so should be read while carrying out the instruction.

The Market Square, now a small car park, was probably laid out during the thirteenth century, as part of an attempt to turn the settlement at Swindon into a market town. High Street, which adjoins it on its west side, as well as Wood Street and Newport ('the new market') Street, are probably also part of this exercise in medieval town planning. The market seems not to have flourished until it was revived after 1626, but thereafter it competed with Highworth as the principal cattle market in north-east Wiltshire. This revitalized market place had a covered market cross in the centre, which was demolished in 1793.

In common with many other small towns at the time, Swindon in the nineteenth century tried to make its market more attractive for farmers and corn dealers. A market house was begun on the south side of the square in 1852, replacing a depot for long-distance waggons (which the railway had made redundant). This market house is the classical building, of which only the shell remains, seen to the right of the tower, but although its upper floor was used for its intended purpose as a town hall, the ground floor never became a covered market, and its arches were filled in for shops. Instead a new

corn exchange with an Italianate tower was built to the left of it in 1864-6. After some fifty years the building became a skating rink and later a cinema and bingo hall. The motto over the door, 'Blessed be the Lord who daily loadeth us with benefits' is perhaps more appropriate to a corn exchange than to a bingo hall. The whole complex is currently (2005) empty and derelict, and the tower is in poor condition.

Opposite these buildings of Bath and Swindon stone, on the north side is a smart eighteenth-century brick house, Square House. And to the east runs Dammas Lane, which was formerly built up with small houses. The name is supposed to derive from damsons, as the lane led to the manor house orchards. The adjacent Saxon Court, a modern housing development, occupies the area in which Saxon huts were discovered and excavated, and so may represent the centre of the settlement which preceded medieval Swindon.

Face the corn exchange and walk past it along High Street to its right, and beyond the modern building. Turn left and walk across the car park to the lane called The Planks. Walk along this lane, past the auction rooms, until the lane bears right in front of a tree-lined grassed area. Here turn left and walk up the path into the public park known as the Lawn. Explore the remains of the manor house gardens adjoining the locked churchyard of Holy Rood on your right. (Wheelchair users will find it easier to turn right from the Market Square into High Street, and then turn right again between ornamental gate piers along the tree-lined path to the Lawn. The churchyard is away to the right.)

The Planks is supposedly derived from a dialect name for flagstones, and it leads towards the site of a mill demolished in about 1860. The mill, which stood below the churchyard, was fed by a spring called Church Well and turned by an extremely large overshot water wheel standing more than thirty feet high. The spring was also used as a water supply, and still feeds the lakes which lie at the southern end of the Lawn, below the church.

'The Lawn' is the name given not only to the area of wooded landscape parkland which separates Old Swindon from the twentieth-century suburbs of Lawn, Park and Walcot, but was also used for the manor house which stood within it until it was demolished in 1952. A sunken garden survives with balustrades, which lay immediately west of the house. The house itself was of brick and stone, and rather similar in style to a surviving house (42, Cricklade Street) which we shall see presently. The Lawn was earlier called Swindon House, and was until 1931 the home of the Goddard family, manorial owners of High Swindon. It presumably occupied the site of the principal (or demesne) house of Swindon's medieval owners before the planned town was created in the thirteenth century.

The adjoining (locked) churchyard contains the chancel and part of the nave arcade of Holy Rood Church. This was Swindon's parish church from the middle ages until 1851, when Christ Church was completed. The author Richard Jefferies was baptized here in 1849. By this date it consisted of a mixture of medieval work and eighteenth-century repairs, which included a new brick tower. But the whole structure was in poor repair – 'hopelessly out of condition, and there being really nothing worth restoring', according to an author who remembered it very well – so that the new church was built, and Holy Rood was allowed to deteriorate. The tower was demolished, and re-erected to its original proportions as a kind of gazebo on a mound not far away; the chancel was restored in 1964, but is now boarded up.

Our tour will leave the Lawn now but, if time permits, a stroll around the parkland to see the lakes, the avenue or 'Long Walk' where Gideon Mantell walked with his 'first love', and since his day the view across suburban Swindon, will be amply rewarded.

From the churchyard area walk towards the brick gazebo tower, and about halfway between them you will encounter a substantial path. Turn left along this and follow it to the exit from the Lawn, which is by a long avenue of young oak trees (planted in 1992 to replace storm-damaged trees). This emerges into High Street between a pair of ornamental gatepiers. Stop at this point to examine the architecture of the street.

We have suggested that the area between the former manor house, the churchyard and the market square is probably the site of the Saxon and early medieval village of Swindon. The market square and High Street represent a planned addition, tacked on to the west of the village. Although the present buildings lining the High Street are not medieval they occupy sites within rectangular tenements which were probably laid out during the thirteenth century. The avenue which takes us back to High Street presumably occupies one such tenement. It was created as the main entrance into the Goddard's park, and originally had lodge houses on each side, as well as the surviving gatepiers.

The row of buildings opposite, along the western side of High Street, dates from the sixteenth to the nineteenth century, and is typical north Wiltshire small-town architecture. From left to right, the Bell has a Victorian facade with a huge bell, but retains traces of an earlier galleried inn behind, and claims to date from 1515. Four doors along, at No.16, notice 'GH' and the date 1631 on the rainwater heads. Old Town Court, now Barclays, proclaims 'Bowly Brewer' above its semicircular arch. Bowly during the 1860s took over the North Wilts Brewery, behind High Street, from John Henry Harding

Sheppard, who gave his four names to streets built on his land in New Swindon which we shall encounter later. No.4, Eastcott House, is the former King of Prussia Inn, and may date from the 17th century; the corner shop has a date of 1708 and the letters 'MH'.

From the gatepiers turn right along High Street, and cross by the pedestrian crossing. Continue to the corner, cross Wood Street, and carry straight on down the hill until you find yourself opposite the entrance to Christ Church. Read the following paragraphs as you go.

Opposite the junction with Wood Street stands Old Swindon's principal inn, the Goddard Arms. The site had earlier been occupied by one of the town's manor houses, and then a thatched inn called the Crown. The present creeper-clad building dates from the eighteenth century. The character of Wood Street is that of a successful Victorian shopping street, and derives from the prosperity which accrued to Old Town traders during the mid-nineteenth century, before New Swindon had developed its own shopping streets. A directory of 1848 claimed that Old Swindon's shops were 'assuming an appearance equal to those of Bath and Cheltenham'. But a few years earlier it had been lined by poor labourers' thatched cottages and blacksmith's forges, producing intolerable noise and smoke, according to Jefferies. It was sometimes called Blacksmiths' Street, or alternatively Windmill Street, because of a windmill which occupied a site near the King's Arms. On the corner the former Wilts and Dorset Bank building of 1884 occupies the site of Blackford's butcher's shop. Members of the Blackford family were champion backsword players, a game which involved clubbing an opponent's head with a wooden stick until the blood ran one inch.

Beyond the Wood Street junction the road continues northward as Cricklade Street, although its old name was Brock Hill. It soon begins to descend the hillside, and a long view over Swindon's northern suburbs opens up. Until a fatal coaching accident in the early nineteenth century the road was carried more abruptly over the brow of the hill, on a level with the present pavement on the Christ Church side. After the accident the gradient was eased for the safety of wheeled vehicles, but not without complaints from the owner of the grand house at the top of the hill. This, No. 42 Cricklade Street (until recently a solicitors' office, but boarded up since 2002), is generally regarded as the finest piece of domestic architecture in Swindon. Sir John Betjeman called it 'one of the most distinguished town houses in Wiltshire'. It was built in 1729, and was occupied as a private house by members of leading Swindon families, including Harding and

Vilett, before becoming the county court and
offices.

Further down the hill an inscription records
a bequest by Alexander Anderson which paid for
a group of four almshouses next to the
churchyard in 1877. Christ Church was designed
by Sir George Gilbert Scott in Midlands
Decorated style, and was opened in 1851. The
hillside site was donated by Ambrose Goddard,
lord of the manor, and the lofty spire, which is
such a prominent feature of the Swindon
townscape, was copied from the genuinely
medieval spire at Buckworth near Huntingdon.
'So new, so high, so pure, so broach'd, so tall', it
presides over the peal of ten bells celebrated in
verse by Betjeman.

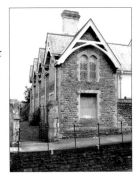

Opposite Christ Church turn left into Church Road, which later becomes
Union Row. When this emerges into the main road (Victoria Road) turn
left, cross by the pedestrian crossing, and make your way back up towards
Old Town. At the T-junction and mini-roundabout at the top of Victoria
Road follow the pavement around to the right, so that you find yourself in
the garden of Apsley House, Swindon Museum.

The siting of Christ Church on Brock Hill must
have improved the status of what had been the
poor end of Old Swindon. A street of meagre
cottages called Little London ran down from the
west end of Wood Street to join Brock Hill where
it bends shortly below Christ Church. This is no
longer built up, and now has the appearance of
a back alley. Church Road crosses it, and then
meets Albert Street, which retains some of its
1840s stone cottages, but not its notorious pub,
the Rhinoceros Inn, which stood at this crossing
until it was demolished in 1963. Albert Street
and Victoria Street (as the upper end of Victoria
Road was originally known) result from Old
Swindon's growth during the 1840s, and are the
counterpart of the railway village at the foot of
the hill. If, when you have crossed the
pedestrian crossing in Victoria Road, you look
back across the road, you will see a quite
distinguished terrace of stone houses (as
opposed to the later and meaner brick houses
beyond the Union Row turning). On no.93 at
first floor level a plaque records that this was
the home of Richard Jefferies, the Wiltshire
naturalist and country writer, from 1875-7.

Walking up Victoria Road to its junction it is
important to realise that, despite its present
importance as the main road between Old and
New Swindon, this link was not established until
about 1875, as the towns began to coalesce.
Earlier ways down the hill were by Brock Hill
and Little London, as we have seen, and by
Eastcott Hill, which we shall use later. Victoria
Street ended merely in a footpath across fields,
by way of Prospect (beyond the present BBC
Wiltshire building).

At the top of Victoria Road, as our footpath leads us round the corner into Bath Road, it is time to take stock. Swindon's medieval street plan was roughly a square of four streets. We have walked along the eastern side of this square (High Street), and looked along Wood Street, the northern side. Now we are at the north-western corner, and the western side is represented by Devizes Road. This was known as Short Hedge until the nineteenth century, and was not built up to any great extent. But we are standing at pre-Victorian Swindon's growth point. Between the 1820s and 1850 housing had begun to creep from this junction southward along Devizes Road, northward along Victoria Street, and westward along what was then called The Sands, but is now Bath Road. Among the first of the new arrivals (probably by 1830) was Apsley House, which has been home to Swindon Museum since 1930. A larger and later development was Bath Terrace, the long row of shops opposite the top of Victoria Road.

Swindon Museum and Art Gallery includes interesting displays of local history, archaeology and palaeontology, as well as important fine art and ceramics collections. Admission is free.

Walk along Bath Road, keeping on the right hand side until you reach the Methodist Church.

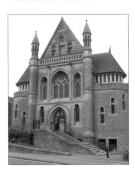

Bath Road is the fashionable nineteenth-century extension to Old Swindon, and its houses display a pleasing variety of styles, using brick, local stone, and occasionally Bath stone. After Apsley House the earliest are the attractive brick houses (now offices) with cast-iron porches, nos.8-14; they date from about 1835, and so are pre-railway. But on the other side of the road, and further along on both sides, the villas are decidedly Victorian, and mostly date from the 1850s and 1860s. The chapel was opened in 1880, and replaced earlier buildings in the Planks.

At this point there is a choice. If you intend to continue the tour by walking down the hill and exploring New Swindon, stay on the right hand side of Bath Road and walk to the corner of Eastcott Road. Resume the description on page 95. If, however, you wish to postpone New Swindon for another occasion and to return to the starting point at the Market Square, cross the road by the pedestrian crossing just beyond the chapel, and continue along Bath Road (away from Old Town) until you reach Quarry Road. Turn left down Quarry Road and, after about 100 yards, enter the Town Gardens by iron gates on your right.

The botanical and horticultural pleasures of the Town Gardens are beyond the scope of this guide, but their historical interest lies in their origins as quarries. The gardens, and the surrounding residential streets, occupy the area of medieval Swindon's Great Field. From the seventeenth century quarries were opened up in parts of this field, at first to win Purbeck

limestone, and later the Portland stone with
which much of Old Swindon is built. Quarrying
declined in the later nineteenth century, and
the Town Gardens were laid out as a public park
in 1894. Their design makes full and attractive
use of the different levels which resulted from
quarrying activities. Near the bandstand is a
polygonal refreshment kiosk. This was built by
the GWR in Swindon works in 1914 for
advertising purposes at local shows, and later
sold to the borough council.

Make your way through the park to its main entrance in Westlecot Road.
Cross the road and turn left. Walk along Westlecot Road until you reach
the parapet of a railway bridge, and see the deep railway cutting below
you. Unless you are a wheelchair user (in which case continue along
Westlecot and Springfield Roads, left into Croft Road, right into Newport
Street, and so back to the start), turn right into Bowling Green Lane, and
immediately you will find a footpath sloping down the side of the cutting.
On the floor of the cutting turn back sharp right, so that you walk under
the railway bridge. Continue in the cutting, and under another bridge,
until you emerge into a small industrial estate.

You are walking along part of the Midland and
South Western Junction Railway line, which ran
from Cheltenham to Southampton. This portion,
with a station serving Old Town known as
Swindon Town, was opened in 1881-2, and
closed in 1961; the site of the station has
become the industrial estate, and a mural
painting reminds us of its former use. While
walking in the cutting look for exposures of
Swindon stone.

Take a left turn (Dewell Mews) out of the industrial estate, and through an
estate of new houses, which have been built on the site of the cattle
market. You will emerge into Marlborough Road next to a bronze statue of
a ram. Turn left, and the town hall, corn exchange and Market Square are
on your right.

The tour to New Swindon resumes at the corner of Bath Road and Eastcott
Road. Turn right into Eastcott Road and follow it as it bends around the
bus depot and begins to descend the hill. At this point it becomes Eastcott
Hill. Cross to the left hand side of Eastcott Hill before you reach the main
road at the bottom (Crombey Street), so that you can use the pedestrian
crossing. Once across Crombey Street continue along the last short stretch
of Eastcott Hill. Cross Commercial Road with care (it has no pedestrian
crossing at this point, and is a fast and busy one-way street) and stop in
front of the town hall in Regent Circus.

The descent down Eastcott Hill two hundred
years ago would have taken us from the
limestone hill of small-town Swindon, with its
arable fields and its quarries, down to the flat,
sparsely populated, clay pasturelands on the
valley floor. This area, the northern portion of
Swindon parish, was generally known as
Eastcott, and was farmed from Upper and Lower
Eastcott Farms. Upper Eastcott Farm stood close
to the later Regent Circus, and had a small
hamlet of cottages around it; Lower Eastcott
Farm lay beneath the site of the present bus
station. Eastcott Road and Eastcott Hill preserve

the course (including the bend) of the lane which connected Swindon with Eastcott, and provided the main link between Old and New Swindon until Victoria Road was created in about 1875.

During the later nineteenth century the houses of New Swindon spread southward up the hill towards the old town, and Old Swindon expanded northward to meet them. Until 1900 the two communities were administered separately, and the boundary between them crossed at the point where Eastcott Road (Old Swindon) turns into Eastcott Hill (New Swindon). Therefore the first side streets which we encounter – King William Street, South Street and North Street on our right, Lansdown Road on our left – are all part of Old Swindon's growth, and date from about 1870. North Street, as its name suggests, marks the northern limit of Old Swindon. But the next streets on our left – Brunswick, Pembroke and Savernake Streets – do not need to respect the boundary because they are a piece of later infilling; they date from 1906-7, after the two towns had amalgamated.

As we descend the hill the small streets to our right date from the 1870s and 1880s, and on our left we encounter Stafford Street and Dixon Street. As a speculative venture they were planned and laid out in 1873, but fell victim to the recession at the works and in the country, and were only patchily built up until the late 1880s. As soon as we pass the end of Dixon Street, however, we emerge from the recession, and find ourselves in a much larger piece of town development, resulting from the boom of the 1890s. The parallel Crombey Street and Commercial Road were the linchpins of the scheme, and numerous short residential roads lead off them at right angles. At the point where Commercial Road and Regent Street would have intersected Regent Circus was laid out, and this, with its imposing brick town hall of 1890-1, was Swindon in its most confident and optimistic mood. But not over-confident, it should be made clear – the original plan, to call it Trafalgar Square, was rejected as being too pretentious.

The town hall was designed in 'Danish Renaissance' style by an architect from Ipswich, Brightwen Binyon, and was originally built as the offices of the New Swindon Local Board. It became the headquarters of Swindon Borough Council when it was incorporated in 1900, but was replaced by new Civic Offices in Euclid Street in 1938. Since 1949 it has housed the central public library, and now includes also a dance studio.

From Regent Circus walk down Regent Street, since 1965 largely pedestrianized, as far as the crossroad with the Parade and Canal Walk.

Regent Street began life as a track through
fields, which connected the hamlet of Eastcott
(in the Regent Circus and Theatre Square area)
with the Golden Lion Bridge across the canal. Its
first building was a Primitive Methodist Chapel,
which opened near the Eastcott end in 1849; a
later brick hall behind its site may still be seen
down an alleyway on the left. During the 1850s
terraces of small brick houses were built along
this track, and it was regarded as a continuation
of Bridge Street. F H Spencer, whom we
encountered in chapter 5, was born in one such
terrace, York Place, which is now concealed
behind shopfronts facing Regent Circus. As
Swindon grew, so there was the need for a more
convenient shopping centre than Old Town on
the hill, and during the 1870s and 1880s most
of the houses along this part of Bridge Street
were converted to shops; to emphasise its new
importance it was renamed Regent Street after
the famous London street.

As you walk down Regent Street look above
the modern shopfronts. At the upper end of the
street, and especially opposite Woolworths, the
roofs of the original small houses may be seen,
and there is a pleasant variety of later
architectural styles. Notice, for instance, the
name W.W. Hunter picked out in ornamental
brickwork; he was a furniture dealer at the turn
of the century, who also built two roads,
Hunters Grove and St Mary's Grove (his wife was
Mary), north of the railway line. On the left side
going down a modern development (datestone
1999) has replaced McIlroys, a local department
store and notable landmark for generations of
Swindonians.

Beyond Edgeware Road much of Regent
Street has been redeveloped in recent years,
and the left hand side forms part of the Brunel
Centre, which was opened in 1972. The
pedestrian crossroad marks the site of the
Golden Lion Inn, with its bridge across the
Wilts and Berks Canal. The line of the canal is
preserved by Canal Walk and the Parade, and a
replica golden lion statue, erected in 1978,
stands nearby. Near the lion, at the entrance to
Messrs Wallis, notice a stone canal milestone
(now a listed building), which gives the
distance to Semington, 26 miles. Semington,
near Melksham in west Wiltshire, is the point at
which the Wilts and Berks Canal joined the
Kennet and Avon. The Parade, as envisaged
during the 1950s, was intended as a road for
vehicles, but this plan was abandoned during
the vogue for separating pedestrians and traffic
which emerged around 1960, and so it was
developed during the early 1960s as Swindon's
first pedestrian precinct.

Having walked down Regent Street turn left along Canal Walk, and keep going. Do not be alarmed that your path takes you through and under a multi-storey car park, and under two road bridges. Continue until you reach the next bridge, Cambria Bridge, which displays children's murals of animals.

The Wilts and Berks Canal, as we saw in chapter 3, was built to link the Bristol and Bath area with the River Thames and London. The Swindon portion was completed in 1804 and the canal was opened throughout in 1810. At that time, and for several decades afterwards, the stretch along which you are walking passed open countryside on both sides, with only a distant view of civilization in the shape of Old Swindon on the hill to the left. During the development of New Swindon after 1840 the canal acted as a barrier, and influenced the way in which the street plan evolved. By the 1890s the canal's useful life was over, and its course through Swindon was both an inconvenience and a health hazard. In 1914 Swindon Borough Council purchased the Swindon portion, together with Coate Water, and the canal's course through the town was filled in.

This stretch of the walk provides a good illustration of how modern Swindon's shopping centre has been superimposed on the earlier pattern of residential streets and small terraced houses. Between Regent Street and the car park all is brash and modern, the shopfronts reflecting the 1970s Brunel Plaza (with 1990s facelift) and the office block, the 22-storey Murray John Tower. But beyond the car park and road bridges is a world of private back gardens and Victorian brick. The smaller, earlier houses are to the right of the canal; to the left Curtis Street and its neighbours date from the building boom of the more affluent 1890s, and their houses are consequently larger and better appointed.

Do not walk under Cambria Bridge, but instead turn right into Cambria Bridge Road, and shortly left into Cambria Place. Halfway along, noting Cambria Baptist Chapel to your left, turn right and you will emerge into Faringdon Road, opposite the former GWR Park.

The tour now moves away from the canal to the world of the early railway settlement. We saw in chapter 5 that a rolling mill for iron rails was built at the works in 1860-1. To construct and operate it workmen from South Wales were encouraged to move with their families to Swindon. At first they were accommodated in the former lodging-house known as the Barracks, but by 1864 two rows of stone cottages, Cambria Place and Cambria Buildings (the south side of Faringdon Road), had been built for them. The project, which has been dubbed 'the second railway village', was perhaps financed by a block mortgage from a building society; at the heart of the community was the Welsh-speaking Baptist chapel, opened in 1866.

When this Welsh colony was established the line of Faringdon Road already existed, and had done for centuries as a track called the 'Fleetway'; indeed private housing was already springing up along it further to the west. To the north of 'Fleetway' a field was given to the GWR by the lord of Eastcott manor in 1844 in order to create a cricket ground and park, and this became the venue every August for a children's fete of gigantic proportions. The park was given by the GWR to the borough council in 1925, in exchange for land elsewhere which the company needed in order to extend the works. Beyond the park is visible the spire of St Mark's Church. This church was completed in 1845, and became the centre of Anglican worship for the railway village and burgeoning new town.

Turn right and walk along the right hand side of Faringdon Road until you have crossed Maxwell Street. Use the pedestrian crossing to cross Faringdon Road, and continue along the left hand side. The terraces of stone cottages which make up the railway village are now on your left, and in due course you will arrive at the centrepiece of the village, Emlyn Square.

The circumstances and evolution of Swindon railway village are described in chapter four, especially pages 47-54, and need not be repeated here. Having refreshed your memory you should stroll around the village, noting especially the lack of uniformity of detail between one terrace and another, the areas of more prestigious housing at the ends of terraces, and the rear alleys (partly necessitated by the lack of mains drainage and sewerage when they were built). You will also see, in Faringdon Road and Emlyn Square, the larger communal buildings, including the former GWR Medical Fund hospital, the baths and swimming pool, the barracks for unmarried workers and the currently disused and sadly dilapidated mechanics' institute.

Walk to the far end of Emlyn Square, beyond the mechanics' institute, and you will find the 'tunnel' entrance, which gave access from the village to the works, beneath the railway lines. Walk through the tunnel and beyond it up the slope to the left, into what is now known as the Great Western Historic Area. Follow the signs across this area to the entrance of the Designer Outlet Village.

The subway or 'tunnel' dates from the building of the carriage works in 1870 between the village and the original railway works buildings. In its heyday it was used by thousands of employees on their way to and from work. The impressive building at its northern end, which housed the GWR administration and drawing office, is now occupied by English Heritage as its National Monuments Record Centre, and welcomes visitors to its exhibitions. Although

parts of the building date from Brunel's time, it was repeatedly enlarged, particularly in 1904-6 . As you make your way across this area you will encounter various buildings of the former railway works, and some newcomers. These include Churchward House, the former works manager's office, with parallel railway lines (known as a traversing table) in front of it. Next to this is STEAM, the Museum of the Great Western Railway (and an essential destination for anyone interested in Swindon's railway heritage), which incorporates a wall of Brunel's original engine house, and other buildings of the 1840s. Opposite are the futuristic new offices of the National Trust, opened in 2005. The McArthur Glen Designer Outlet Centre is accommodated in locomotive's works buildings, mostly dating from the great expansion of the 1870s and incorporates the brass foundry, machine and boiler shops. Opened in 1997 Its success has contributed to Swindon's regeneration and optimism for the future.

After the distraction of museums and bargain hunting retrace your steps to the tunnel. When you emerge turn left and then right into Emlyn Square, then cross and turn left into Oxford Street. At the far end of Oxford Street cross East Street and continue along Harding Street towards the Express by Holiday Inn. Turn right immediately beyond this hotel into Bridge Street.

East Street signals the end of the railway village, and the beginning of Sheppard's Field. John Henry Harding Sheppard was the successful Old Town brewer who gave each of his names to a street in this area around 1870. The terraces of cottages which covered his field have now, for the most part, been cleared, and much of the site has been redeveloped. In front of you large modern office blocks now fill the area between the railway station (away to your left) and the shopping centre (to your right).

We have already encountered the southern end of the original Bridge Street (which became Regent Street). Now we are standing at the northern end, which led to the point where the North Wilts Canal, having branched off from the Wilts and Berks, ran beneath the railway lines. Like Regent Street, this part of Bridge Street was built up with terraced housing during the 1850s, and some was later converted to commercial use.

Walk along Bridge Street to its junction with Fleet Street (where it becomes pedestrianized) and turn left. At the end of Fleet Street the road emerges into a townscape of traffic and large office blocks. Turn right and follow the pathway until you reach the underpass, which takes you beneath Fleming Way to the bus stops on the far side.

Fleet Street, of course, takes its name from 'Fleetway', the early track which we encountered further along as Faringdon Road. Like Bridge Street it was built up during the 1850s, and a few early cottages remain. Fleming Way, by contrast, is a relatively modern creation, built in 1958 to divert traffic away from the new shopping centre. It takes its name from Harold Fleming, Swindon Town Football Club's star player between 1907 and 1924, and an England cap. He died in 1955.

Fleming Way follows the line of the North Wilts Canal, which had a long and stormy gestation period before its opening in 1819. It was built to connect the Wilts and Berks Canal with the Thames and Severn, and had the effect of enabling canal traffic to by-pass the supposedly navigable upper reaches of the Thames or Isis, from Lechlade through Oxford to Abingdon. As we saw in chapter 3, it was the existence of these canals which gave Swindon the 'first push' on its way to becoming the large and important town which it is today. And the junction of the North Wilts with the Wilts and Berks Canals, as you stand and wait for your bus back up to Old Town, is precisely under your feet.

At the time of writing (2005) buses no.10 (to Okus, from stand V) and 11 (to the Great Western Hospital, from stand U) operate daytime services to Old Town from Fleming Way, every 30 and 15 minutes, respectively. If you prefer to walk back up the hill do not use the underpass but continue along Fleming Way and turn right at the first roundabout into Princes Street. This becomes Clarence Street and then Victoria Road. At the top of Victoria Road turn left into Wood Street, and then right into High Street. From Fleming Way to Old Town Market Square is about a mile, mostly uphill.

DELVING DEEPER

A SHORT BOOK SUCH AS THIS cannot do justice to a subject as large as Swindon. Whole areas of great interest have been entirely omitted, or merely mentioned in passing. But if this book has succeeded in its aim of fuelling your interest in local history, there are several things which you could do next to unravel more of the Swindon code.

A good starting point would be a visit to STEAM, the recently opened GWR museum housed in a building of the former railway works. This and the Swindon Museum in Bath Road, Old Town, have displays and artefacts which will enable you to learn more about the town's history. The National Monuments Record Centre also has a programme of exhibitions, and is involved in local history activities.

To research Swindon's history the Local Studies section of the Swindon Reference Library will be your first port of call. The books listed below, and many others, are available there, and some of them can also be found in other public libraries in Swindon. The Reference Library will also be able to give you up-to-date information about local history and similar societies, such as the Swindon Society, and activities in Swindon which you may wish to join and attend. An excellent example of such a group currently at work is the Rodbourne Living Story Project. The Central Library will be moving soon to temporary premises to allow it to be rebuilt on the same site, and the new library when it reopens will include improved facilities for local and family history study.

Most archival sources are held in the Wiltshire and Swindon Record Office, at present (2005) in Trowbridge, but it will be moving to state-of-the-art prermises on a site near Chippenham railway station in 2007. A great deal can also be learned about Swindon's history from websites of local and national origin.

Listed below are some of the most important published books about the history of Swindon, and these have been heavily used in the writing of the present short history.

Ball, Felicity, and Bryan, Tim, *Swindon and the GWR*, 2003

Boddy, Martin, and others, *City for the 21st century: globalisation, planning and urban change*, 1997

Cattell, John, and Falconer, Keith, *Swindon: the legacy of a railway town*, 1995

Chandler, C.J., and others,*'Off the map of history'? the development of north-east Wiltshire to 1600*, 1989

Child, Mark, *Swindon: an illustrated history*, 2002

Crittall, Elizabeth, and others, *A history of Swindon to 1965*, 1983 [reprinted from the *Victoria History of Wiltshire*, vol.9, 1970]

Grinsell, L.V., and others, *Studies in the history of Swindon*, 1950 [includes John Betjeman's essay on Swindon architecture]

Harloe, Michael, *Swindon: a town in transition*, 1975

Hudson, John and Linda, *Swindon in the news*, 2002

Hudson, Kenneth, *An awkward size for a town: a study of Swindon at the 100,000 mark*, 1967

Lindley, Kenneth, *Town time and people*, 1962

Jefferies, Richard, *Jefferies' land: a history of Swindon and its environs...* edited with notes by Grace Toplis, 1896

Large, Frederick, *A Swindon retrospect, 1855-1930*, 1932

Morris, William, *Swindon fifty years ago (more or less): reminiscences, notes and relics of ye old Wiltshire towne*, 1885 [new edition 1970]

Peck, Alan S., *The Great Western at Swindon Works*, 1983

Silto, William, *Of stone and steam: the story of Swindon railway village*, 1989

Williams, Alfred, *Life in a railway factory*, 1915

INDEX

Please note that the Journey of Discovery, chapter 8, has not been indexed, and minor references have been omitted.

ROUTE MAP

This map is designed to help you follow chapter 8, A Journey of Discovery, around Old and New Swindon. The route is explained on pages 89 to 101 above, and the numbers included on the map along the way refer to the page numbers above where instructions are given. Good luck!

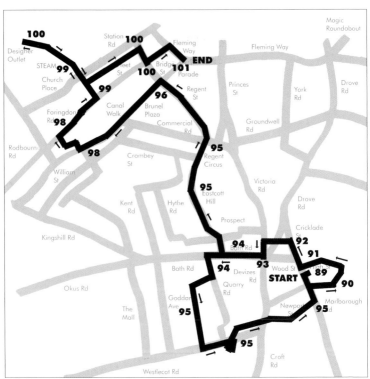